REAL

A PATH TO PASSION, PURPOSE, AND PROFITS
IN REAL ESTATE

FOR MY PARENTS

Who taught a little hellion that falling down
is ok as long as you get back up.

And for my wife, Lisa, and daughters
Taylor, Amber, Kaydee, and Jessica,
who have learned through all
of life's ups and downs right beside me.

World change starts with educated and healthy children. We support programs that expand literacy, gender equality and science research.

20% of royalties are donated to RoomtoRead.org and the Wylder Nation Foundation.

CONTENTS

DEDICATION TO CRAFT

FOREWORD

Michele Serro

Founder, Doorsteps

Like so many hardworking folks, I began my career dreaming of having some kind of meaningful impact on the world—building something interesting, something important, something needed, something that would begin as mine, quickly become ours, and with luck would one day become everyone's.

My connection with real estate began in 2006 when I bought my first home in New York City. Suffice it to say, the buying process was painful and jarring, and I could not understand why on earth it needed to be that way. If the experience of making a home for yourself and your family is so important and so profoundly human, it only follows logic that the experience of buying one should be, too. I remember saying to myself, if Jeff Bezos can make buying a book a delightful experience, why not do the same with a home? Although I was right to want a better experience, I was incredibly naive about the true complexities of effectuating a real estate transaction.

But like so many things in our lives, when there is something you need to learn, the same situation will repeat itself until you grasp the lesson or accomplish your goal. In 2010, I went through the buying process a second time, and it was just as bad, if not worse, than the first go. At the time I was working at IDEO, a leading design firm, and my experiences there led me to understand why the real estate process was so bad. Most systems tend towards the complex and fragmented, with multiple stakeholders and misaligned incentives. Real estate is a system. Add to that the fact that buying a house is one of the most emotional purchases in a lifetime—clearly, there is nothing "one-click" about it.

My time at IDEO taught me to take a critical look at accepted models and seek opportunities to make them better. And I thought homebuying could be better. Like any good designer, in order to effect meaningful change, I had to first gain true empathy for the people, the system, and the players I was looking to help. So, I quit my job at the world's most respected design consultancy and went on a quest to learn and respect real estate and all of its little quips and quirks.

After months of research and conversations, it was clear that the real estate agent, one of the most important actors in buying a home, was at a constant disadvantage. When transactions go smoothly, an agent's value is easily overlooked. However, when things go wrong, the agent is the first to be blamed, despite significant investment of time and effort. Because of where they sit within an incredibly complex system, the impact of an agent's work is literally obscured. So it was not surprising to me to see so many agents become a product of their environment, getting too wrapped up in the transactional side of things, chasing the next sale instead of building long-term relationships, because, well, a sale translates to survival.

In taking on the home-buying process and with this in mind, I knew it would be vital to reframe the industry's notion of service to create a better environment for agents. Moreover, such a shift would increase expectations on the part of the consumer, providing clarity about the experience and the ability to ask for service. I believed a different mindset could begin to change the industry.

I connected to so many of the thoughts and stories in this book, but most significantly to the idea that real estate is not just a job, but a craft—your craft. Why think about real estate as a craft? A craft is honed over a lifetime; even a master craftsman has skills to refine and new knowledge to acquire. Within a craft system, there is always room to improve and to derive personal satisfaction from the process and end result.

So, what exactly, is the true craft of real estate? Dave, Lani, Martin, and all of the contributors to this book have touched on many of the things that shape the craft of real estate. Distilled to their simplest, most vital components, they are *skill, knowledge,* and *passion.*

Whether learned through study or developed through experience, skill justifies the need for increased specialization. This precept is not about training to do a job with your eyes closed, it is about honing a craft in order to make a difference and build something meaningful. Mastery results from constant repetition.

Knowledge is both theoretical and practical, with the latter being most relevant to craft. Applied knowledge enables one to be discerning and particular in their actions, responding to the situation at hand with relevance and value.

Passion is the love of or investment in an art that motivates us to keep practicing and honing our skill. Passion draws us to like-minded people and livelihoods. It creates pride in our work. We find meaning by finding our passion.

Some will wonder where technology is on this short list. Technology can enhance good craftspeople, but it cannot replace them.

Real estate will always require the contribution of smart, invested people motivated by a sense of purpose. Focus on your purpose and your passion. Let passion be the first thing that makes you a good agent. Yell about your love of the craft from the rooftops, let your zeal shine in your emails, recognize your dedication in your conversations when you become everyone's favorite agent. Because actual passion—messy, unapologetic passion—is something undeniable that no one (most importantly, you) can diminish or dispute. Helping people find their way home is important, rewarding, and life-changing work.

START HERE

"It is every man's obligation to put back into the world
at least the equivalent of what he takes out of it."
– Albert Einstein

It's a sizzling Phoenix, Arizona afternoon in August, 2006. My wife and children are splashing in the pool while I man the grill. I'm ensconced in a shady spot, keeping watch over the burgers and dogs, and while the shade provides some respite, the daytime temperature remains 112°. Describing an Arizona summer as "hot" is a gross understatement—the breeze on your face feels like sticking your head in a convection oven.

"Who wants cheese?," I yell out.

Making a cheeseburger in the summertime in Phoenix requires a bit of planning. The final assembly must be expertly timed. You can't keep the cheese outside on standby or it will melt and stick to whatever surface it is on. Instead, the burgers have to be very nearly ready so you can sprint to the fridge, grab the Cheddar Jack, rush back, top the patties, and achieve a nice melt before lunch is incinerated.

Armed with a beer in one hand and a spatula in the other, Fleetwood Mac on the speakers, and the blissful sound of my children playing, I seemingly don't have a care in the world—except for the cheeseburgers. Indeed, my real estate business is booming. That particular month marked my tenth year in real estate and the third consecutive month of record personal income. I had grossed just over $80,000 in commissions the month prior and nearly $50,000 in revenue the month before that. I have roughly 25 active listings, with four in escrow, and stand to earn $40,000 from those sales alone. It seems unreal that, a scant eight years ago, I had to call my wife and tell her we were broke because multiple closings had disintegrated, thus vaporizing my earnings.

All in all, things are good. Or so it seems. Actually, I am gripped by anxiety because several escrows are shaky. I can't focus. My problem is deep and insidious, and no matter my facade, my current worries aren't novel. Stress has lingered and nagged me for quite some time. I've ballooned to 230 pounds. I feel miserable. This day spent by the pool with family and friends should be relaxing and wonderful. But it isn't. I simply can't enjoy it.

And that's the real travesty. To this day, the thought of that lost opportunity makes me cringe because I failed to be present. My mind was completely wrapped up with work. And sadly, it was just one instance among many others, such as when my kids were anxious to play or excited to share something personal, or my wife simply hoped to have a sweet and meaningful conversation.

Looking back, now seven years on, it's clear where I went wrong. I was certainly successful, as measured in dollars, but my thinking was flawed. My habits were unsustainable.

I have no hesitation in admitting now that I was plagued with arrogance. As the market started to slip in early 2007, I believed I could outsmart what was to be an obvious and pernicious downturn. When tactics didn't work, I bet that I could outspend the crisis, blanketing television, print, and the web. I held on for a while, perhaps longer than many, but the market buckled regardless. I failed to escape the collapse—professionally and personally. The value of my own home plummeted from $750,000 to $350,000, and with its equity erased, I was forced to short sale the house my wife and I raised our kids in. I went broke. Again. Heartbroken just like millions of other Americans.

It's now 2013. My wife and I have rebuilt our lives again, and I now consider the crash a blessing in disguise. If I had continued treading the same path, I likely would have been dead before fifty. Moreover, although painful, the crash and the six years elapsed since have taught me some invaluable lessons in the real estate business and in life.

I wrote this book and invited other industry veterans to share their stories to prove that no matter the market, the peaks and the dips, one can succeed in real estate. I've ignored the crap of countless self- help books and what cheesy gurus shill on stage to offer the truth. This book doesn't espouse management theories, explain how to bolster curb appeal, or demonstrate how to use Twitter to save your business. Instead, this book shares the collective experience of working with thousands of clients and buying and selling thousands of homes.

I hope that existing agents are encouraged by what is confessed here. I hope new real estate professionals find guidance. I hope that prospective realtors, perhaps even my children's generation, absorb what it really it takes to make it.

Success means different things to different people, so let me be exceedingly clear on my definition. Success is not about money. Success is finding purpose in what you do. Success is an expression of passion, the realization of a sustainable business. Success is contributing to the lives of others. And ultimately, I believe that success is generating enough income to fund your ideal lifestyle, whether it be as a globetrotter, a foster parent, an expert gardener, or a teacher, and never, ever being cornered into missing precious moments in this short life.

If just one person is inspired to make real estate a career, or if just one veteran rekindles their passion for the trade instead of banging their anxiety-riddled head on the wall every day, I would honestly consider this book a success.

— Dave Crumby

HOW TO USE
THIS BOOK

*"Does history record any case in which
the majority was right?"*
– Robert Heinlein

I wrote this book because I feel I have something new to say about what it takes to succeed (or not succeed) in the real estate business.

I believe real estate to be an excellent career choice, and when approached and worked with authenticity and focus, it fuels happy and fulfilling lives. Lives filled with growth and progress; with freedom and flexibility; with connection to the community and with a higher purpose. Even after two recessions, one burst bubble, multiple business models, and countless doom-and-gloom predictions, I still believe.

This book isn't about theories or ideas about how being a real estate agent *should* work. Instead my contributors and I are sharing our extensive, collective experience in the field. The goal of the book is to help existing agents overcome the pitfalls we've experienced collectively and hopefully inspire a new generation to dedicate their lives to the craft of real estate – while giving realistic expectations of what it takes to make it. This book is born from years of pain, of frustration, of joy, of ideas, and we hope to imprint on you our philosophy that we believe will be relevant and practical whether you're reading this book today or in 2063. Our approach is low-tech, simple, and slow, but it is proven.

I purposely divided this book into three main parts, YOU, US, and FORWARD. Some of you may only need the first 100 or so pages to "get it" and start the process of reinventing your approach. Others may want to read from start to finish. Think of this book as a buffet. Take what you would like. Revisit when ready.

Part I, YOU, consists of business and life fundamentals. Just like a house (or any structure), you need a solid foundation to build from. Your business is no different. It requires solid footings to weather the inevitable changes in life and the macro/micro economic forces at work, some of which you have no control over. If your foundation is strong, and you're fueled by passion and purpose, your business will withstand changes and overcome the hurdles.

Part II, US, is a collection of stories from some of the most influential leaders in the real estate industry. This section surprised me as the book took shape, as I found myself again in the role of student, learning from and being inspired by the contributors. What is taught and shared is invaluable, timeless, and I am confident that if you heed the wisdom, you will succeed not only in real estate but in life.

Part III, FORWARD, is the road map I extrapolated from my own experiences and what I learned from the contributors in *Part II*. Inspiration and attention is perishable, so I wanted to include a section you can revisit from time to time for a quick infusion of inspiration. A small portion of the content in this section was inspired and borrowed with permission from Leo Babauta to help plant the seed that a narrow focus can lead to breakthroughs and opportunities you never imagined.

My hope for you is to build a sustainable business. To do this requires new thinking and habits, none more important than having sustained energy and inspiration to shape your vision and purpose your day.

Thank you in advance for investing the time to listen to what my contributors and I have to say. In today's fast paced world, we're truly grateful for your indulgence. We promise to pour it all out, not hold anything back, and deliver value, whether you've been in the business 30 days or 30 years.

With the caliber of people contributing to this book, you're going to learn a lot. But your rewards won't come from merely learning. True joy is creating something and putting it out into the world for other to enjoy. Now let's get started.

YOU

"You only live once,
but if you do it right,
once is enough."

— **Mae West**

PASSION.

PURPOSE.

PROFITS.

*"We don't beat the reaper by living longer.
We beat the reaper by living well."
— Randy Pausch (1960-2008), the last
lecture at Carnegie Mellon*

EVOLVE
YOUR REAL

*"The ache for home lives in all of us, the safe place
where we can go as we are and not be questioned."*
— Maya Angelou

Real estate is important. Whether it's a house, a cabin in the mountains, a piece of family land, or a favorite oceanside escape, where we are at any time has great significance. Real estate's locale, boundaries, and geographical terrain shape cultures, determine livelihoods, and even recollect the past. We spend significant sums of money to visit a tucked away village filled with archeological ruins. We marvel at how mankind transforms it, whether the construction has existed for five thousand years or five days. Ultimately, real estate is the center of our lives. It's where we gather, where we raise our kids, and where we laugh, cry, recover, and rejuvenate. It's about home.

As real estate agents, you and I have the distinct and vital role of guiding people through the transfer of one of the most important pieces of their lives. However, this mantle is often overlooked or is expressed as a platitude. And frankly, the dismissiveness hurts our industry. We sometimes forget how important a role we play in society. People joke about real estate agents—tainting the lens through which our profession is viewed—but we minimize the profession's consequence, too. After we sell a few dozen (or a few hundred) houses, homes are itemized as sales, people into scribbles in an address book, and purpose rusts into the hopeless pursuit of "more" leads, units, and income. Reducing our role to mere tactics, statistics, paperwork, transactions, and dollars not only commoditizes the individuals we're trusted to guide, but it commoditizes our lives, too.

But the role of an agent is vital. Moreover, our career provides unique advantages and opportunities. One simply has to look at other jobs to really appreciate—even fall in love with (again)— what real estate has to offer.

Our culture certainly aggrandizes "more," but its pursuit is a fool's errand. Worse, it comes at great expense to everyone. The culture we've produced pushes people to breaking points with little or no balance. Only ten percent of the population of the United States takes a full two weeks off per year. Most take far less time.

If you look at other first-world countries with roughly the same standard of living as the United States, you'll find that employer paid vacation is mandatory. In fact, it's common for all employees living in Germany, Denmark, France, Italy, and even Great Britain to receive *twenty to twenty-five days* of paid vacation time per year. If you add national holidays, the number of paid days off can eclipse forty. In sharp contrast, the United States is the only country among its peers to not mandate paid vacation of any kind. The average American has just *nine days* of vacation a year.

Does nine days of vacation sound like a good life to you? Likely not. Yet there are, quite literally, millions of people leading lives of quiet desperation, working long and hard hours in jobs they despise, all in hopes of being able to do what they really want to do... "someday." Unfortunately, that someday rarely comes.

Little time off is a symptom of a larger problem. Wrongly, life is treated by so many as a pilgrimage, with some "reward" at the end. Success, we are taught, waits for us at the finish line. But that is a hoax, a terrible hoax. Life is a musical thing. You're supposed to sing, strum, and dance while the music is being played.

"Life deferment" isn't a real estate industry problem—it's a overarching cultural disaster. Instead of seeking an equilibrium with our economic system, we push to work harder, sell more, outsource, downsize, and increase profits (by any means). "More, bigger, faster" is the ethos since the Industrial Revolution. And for what? So we can mortgage our lives, our time with our children, and our passions for the idea that when we retire we can enjoy them?

Consider this question: Do you want to live your life like a mortgagor, with so little spent on what's principal? Or, ignoring the real estate simile, do you want to work and work, making a 160-hour (minimum) payment each and every month, with so little time and energy spent on your passions? The mortgagor and the owner have very different philosophies. Some examples:

The Mortgagor	The Owner
Hopes to retire someday.	Schedules periodic mini-retirements, restorative vacations, and frequent breaks to explore, learn, and grow.
Aims to make lots of money.	Earns enough money to fund an ideal lifestyle and pursue lifelong dreams.
Acquires more and more.	Does more with less and avoids clutter.
Spends gobs of money on full page egocentric ads.	Builds meaningful, ongoing relationships with people and communities.

The bottom line is that if you don't design your life, someone will do it for you, and you may not like their notions and priorities.

Chances are you chose real estate largely because you want to design your own life. You appreciate that we're here for a short time, and if anyone is to dictate how you're going to live, it sure as hell better be you.

Real estate is different. You're in control. You can shape your own destiny. In real estate, you can build an ideal lifestyle, balancing work, joy, and more than two weeks of vacation. If approached with the right attitude, philosophy, and habits, you can create the time, space, and flexibility to fuel a life that others, even lawyers, doctors, and corporate executives would drool over.

But you have to be all in.

I AM

"If you chase two rabbits, both will escape."
– Unknown

I have a confession. For years, when asked what I did for a living, I often hesitated to reply. Whether I feared being judged or being dismissed as a bubble-head, I recoiled anytime I was asked that ice-breaker question. "Realtor" was the last answer I wanted to give. And this sentiment wasn't and isn't unique to me. Such trepidation explains why we euphemize our titles as "Real Estate Consultant," "Forensic Property Analyzer," and "Certified Short Sale Expert."

Let's be honest: the technicalities of real estate aren't exactly on par with those of, say, neurosurgery, nuclear power, or bridge building. The barriers to enter real estate are very low — passing a single class and a state exam is sufficient for licensure — and the old-school brokerage model only succeeds when an office is fully staffed with eager agents. For better or worse, these conditions make it easy for most anyone to "give real estate a try."

Obviously, people that fork over tuition for real estate school have the best intentions, but realty also appeals to those with the "If I can just do one deal a month" mentality. There's nothing wrong with that, if the person is fully invested in the craft. However, the truth is that even infrequent listings and sales require commitment.

Making the commitment to this profession is fundamental and easily the first and most important step to take. Make the decision that real estate *is* your occupation. If you're not prepared to make that decision and commit, no amount of training, from me or anyone else, is going to help you.

I like what Goethe wrote about initiative. I've found his insight to be very true.

"Until one is committed, there is hesitancy, the chance to draw back. Concerning all acts of initiative (and creation), there is one elementary truth that ignorance of which kills countless ideas and splendid plans: that the moment one definitely commits oneself, then Providence moves, too.

"All sorts of things occur to help one that would never otherwise have occurred. A whole stream of events issues from the decision, raising in one's favor all manner of unforeseen incidents and meetings and material assistance, which no man could have dreamed would have come his way.

"Whatever you can do, or dream you can do, begin it. Boldness has genius, power, and magic in it. Begin it now."

Now I'm going to be blunt. Despite the plethora of marketing systems that promise to magically catapult you from a zero to a hero in 45 days, I must assert that building your business is going to take some time. You won't be a big hit right away. You won't make it overnight. You are not so special that your peers will take notice of your every move (at least not yet.) If that's too much of a buzzkill, I'll refund what you paid for this book.

Even on the rare occasion that lightning strikes, bringing instant success, the win is typically ephemeral. Without a foundation, the money or notoriety cannot last. Trust me. I've been there.

Rather, I ask that you trade the dream of overnight success for slow, measured growth and a deliberate plan for a full life. The latter is a difficult option to choose, and I understand patience is a rare commodity, but you have to do the work. Progress will be slow, but sure.

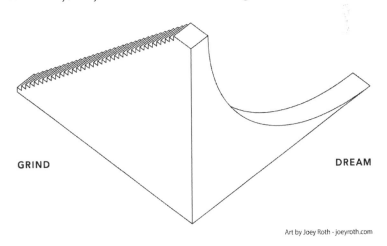

GRIND   DREAM

Art by Joey Roth - joeyroth.com

The figure above captures the difference between the options. The *grind* requires more effort. It is a disciplined, incremental march through reality towards a goal. Compare it to the *dream*, a good idea that loses potency as it encounters reality.

Once you make the decision to make real estate your life's work, you have to adopt the attitude that you are committing to a trade for life.

Conducting a transaction is simple. More difficult is committing yourself for five to ten years to build a sustainable business able to thrive in any market condition. It all comes down to a choice. If you have that patience—I assure you, once you've made the commitment that real estate is your craft—you'll adopt a different mindset and be open to how deep you have to go.

THE CRAFT OF
REAL ESTATE

My family moved to beautiful Denver, Colorado two years ago. During the first few months after the move, I went back and forth to Phoenix to manage my real estate business as I transitioned to my new job as CEO of Realvolve.

One summer night, on my birthday, my family took me to dinner before my flight. One of the things my family loves to do is eat, and one of our favorite meals is sushi. New to the area, we queried Yelp to find recommendations, chose a place, arrived, and sat at the sushi bar in front of one of the chefs.

As my family enjoyed the delicious food and each other's company, I had the feeling I was being watched, studied. The chef deduced it was my birthday, yet instead of the obligatory "Happy Birthday!" sentiment, he discussed the virtues of being a Leo (he was a Leo, too) and described who else in history shared the same astrological sign. After a couple of sakes, the banter made for light and pleasant conversation, yet I felt something was different about him. This man had a quiet energy and wisdom about him, and was humble, yet confident and assertive.

As we concluded our meal, I asked the chef if he owned the restaurant. He chuckled and said, "I am the low man on the totem pole." I thanked him, and he asked for my email address to send periodic dinner specials. I happily shared my details and caught my flight to Phoenix.

Around 1 a.m., I received the following email message:

Hello,

It was a pleasure serving you tonight on your birthday! I hope you had a nice evening!

I'd like to take this opportunity to properly introduce myself. My name is Yasu Kizaki, one of the founders of three restaurants. I am the eldest of four brothers; my second brother, Toshi, is the head of the organization, and is the master chef of all of our restaurants. Our youngest brother lives a few minutes away from the fish market in the city of Fukuoka, located on Kyushu, the southernmost island of Japan. He handpicks the freshest fish from the market and sends them to us.

Apart from making sushi every night, I also take care of public relations, marketing, human resources, and special events, such as the Sushi Class I teach every two weeks. In addition to what I do at the restaurant, on a completely personal level, I help local non-profits raise funding. I normally raise $40,000 a year.

That is all from me this time. I hope your stay in Denver will be a great one. I hope to see you very soon.

Sincerely,
Yasu Kizaki

I was blown away. Although short and somewhat canned, the email was nonetheless specific to our conversation. He recalled fine details about me and took the opportunity to share things about himself. He also shared his "why," or the things that are important to him (more about this shortly).

Did Yasu do anything really remarkable? No. He was an attentive host and many restaurants send email to patrons. However, Yasu was *authentic*. I have since learned that Yasu's Sushi Den is not only one of the top sushi bars in the United States, it's one of the busiest Japanese restaurants in the world. Yet there he was, sending me personal email in the wee hours of the morning.

Yasu has since become an inspiration and something of a muse for me. Indeed, his example was a catalyst for writing this book. What impressed me so? The food, yes, but more so was Yasu's passion. He moved to Denver twenty five years ago with limited resources, knew scant English, and yet was brave enough to open a sushi restaurant. (Not many people were eating sushi 25 years ago, and few if any in Denver.) Yasu followed his heart and follows it to this day. Even after nearly three decades of performing the same functions, he is no less attentive to every piece of sushi and sashimi. Each garners nothing short of his utmost focus. He pays equal attention to his relationships.

Few people in the public would consider real estate a craft and fewer a form of art, but in practice it's a combination of both, not unlike making mouth-watering sushi. Building a successful real estate business requires technical acumen and the artistry of founding and maintaining meaningful relationships.

You can be just like Yasu. Be different. Be authentic. Be real. Be a *shokunin*. A Japanese word, shokunin translates roughly to craftsman or artisan. However, such a literal translation fails to convey its true meaning. A Japanese apprentice is taught that shokunin means having an acumen and an attitude of social consciousness. The shokunin has an obligation to work stridently for the general welfare of the people, be it spiritual or material.

When work, commitment, and pleasure become one, you embody the passion of your craft and nothing is impossible. When you've discovered your purpose, people take notice. They connect to your "why."

THE ART & SCIENCE
OF PEOPLE

*"Arts and sciences are branches of the same tree.
All these aspirations are directed toward ennobling man's
life, lifting it from the sphere of mere physical existence and
leading the individual towards freedom."*
— Albert Einstein

I visited London a few years ago to speak at an Internet marketing conference. On the last day of my trip, I took a train to Paris to visit the Louvre Museum. Among the myriad of stunning and famous works of art in its collection and galleries, the *Mona Lisa*, painted by Leonardo Da Vinci, is undoubtedly the museum's main attraction. (The *Mona Lisa* has been permanently displayed in the Louvre since 1797.)

Contrary to what you might imagine, Da Vinci's oil painting, rendered in the four years between 1503 and 1506, is small, at just 30 inches tall and 21 inches wide. However, what it lacks in size is offset by sizzle. Not only is the workmanship and execution mesmerizing, looking at it conjures up all sorts of questions. Who is the model? Or, who were the *models*? Is the subject smiling? If she is, at what or at whom?

Academics can (and do) argue those questions, but what puzzled me was more practical: How did Da Vinci stay dedicated to the work for such a long time? Did friends criticize his work? Did he get dejected or bored? What if Da Vinci sketched something and a week later said to himself, "Meh, I think I'll go lay on the couch and watch 'Dancing with the Stars'?" Obviously, the world wouldn't have the *Mona Lisa* and would be just slightly less colorful, less enriched. Now further imagine that Da Vinci, Joyce, Bell, Einstein, Twombly, and Jobs had all been lazy. Things would be drab all around.

Fortunately, all those creators and many more stellar talents didn't lie around watching reruns, but persisted, doggedly so, in their individual endeavors. To such creators, failure was not a terminus. It was an origin.

And that mindset makes all the difference in the world. Be it driven by stubbornness, vision, perspiration, or inspiration, perseverance separates the marvelous from the mediocre. There are plenty of painters in the world — and writers, musicians, politicians, doctors, coaches — and plenty of real estate agents, but few ultimately choose to clamber over all the obstacles to truly stand out and make the leap from *salesman* to *craftsman*.

Consider the illustration below. It was inspired by Artist Joey Roth and visually shows the difference between a salesman and a craftsman.

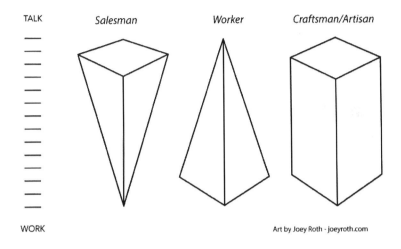

Art by Joey Roth - joeyroth.com

The salesman is showmanship (talk) without substance (work). The worker is substance (work) without panache (talk). The craftsman has both style and substance. Put another way, the artisan has tactics and strategy. And while someone can copy tactics readily, copying a strategy is far from easy. There is a quote from *The Art of War*: "Everyone knows my tactics, but no one knows my strategy."

In real estate, the transaction is our craft. The relationship is our art. And the world is losing our art.

As with any art, there is no absolute formula or shortcut to success in real estate (nor an absolute definition of success). Instead, achievement comes from authenticity. It comes from you being you. Your art is the work required to form and foster relationships month after month, year after year. And it is that art that forms the basis of a sustainable real estate business. Otherwise, selling real estate is just a job, and you are (effectively) unemployed after each and every deal.

Our art is the foundation of our business, and it's one of the most difficult practices to master. Creating, building, and fostering relationships requires you to grow as a human being. You must evolve in every area of life, be it adoption of emerging technologies, adaptation to market conditions, accepting new ideas, or even the embrace of spirituality. Our art requires you to push yourself. And this never ends.

As the graphic below shows, your art (work) is creating something from inspiration, mediated by an uncompromising picture of reality, then launching it with precision into the world.

To be sure, molding pent up inspiration into a creation can induce anxiety. For example, this book has me anxious and vulnerable. This work will be dissected, judged, critiqued, praised, ridiculed, and mocked, just as your great works will be, no matter the size. Ultimately, creating art puts you in a vulnerable position.

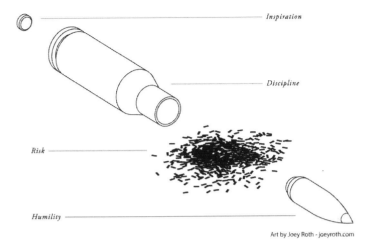

Art by Joey Roth - joeyroth.com

Putting your work into the world starts with an idea (inspiration) and entails discipline and risk. How the world reacts can't be predicted or controlled. But we continue, we learn, we adapt, and our precision improves. All we can do is put our heart and work into the world. It's our art. It's our purpose.

Vision + Art + Science = Breakthrough

In this vulnerable, exposed position, not only are inspiration, discipline, risk, and humility required, heavy lifting is the overarching ingredient required of artisans and craftsman. We can't do that heavy lifting for you, but we can help you understand the science of relationships and point the way to find people who know, like, and trust you.

Establishing a new relationship with another has four key stages.

1. Initially, someone is *aware* of you. The person has heard your name in conversation, seen your advertisement, or has perhaps attended your conference presentation.

2. Next, the person *knows* you. You sat at the same table for lunch, discussed business, compared notes, and traded some personal information.

3. In the third stage of the relationship, the person *likes* you. You have demonstrated who you are and revealed what is important to you and you share some attributes and interests.

4. Finally, the person *trusts* your advice and seeks your counsel. You engage regularly with the person, share expertise and experience, and have demonstrated that you are trustworthy.

The four stages are pictured in the image below.

Most real estate agents focus solely on stage one, awareness, attempting to attract business via advertising, marketing, cold calls, and open houses. The focus is "getting out there." Few expend the energy to advance to stage two or make wrongheaded attempts. For example, many agents employ mass email messages, seeking exposure and more direct contact. However, canned missives do little more than grocery cart ads; in fact, such rote attempts typically generate repulsion, an anathema to relationships.

I'm not suggesting you discard those tools entirely. Just don't expect to build a lasting business built on widgets, gizmos, and gadgets alone. You must engender likability and trustworthiness. To do that, you have to get close to people, in all senses of the word.

In social psychology, *propinquity* explains that a person tends to form relationships with those whom he or she is exposed to often. Or in other words, frequency and familiarity tend to form a bond between one person and another. If you need an example, consider an office. Workplace interactions are frequent; thus, close relationships between coworkers form readily.

You need not work in office to benefit from propinquity. Your neighborhood, place of worship, CrossFit box, community center, or yoga studio can serve just as well.

Real world proximity is *physical propinquity*. Another predictor of close relationships is *psychological propinquity*, or how much views and experiences are shared. Here, the notion is that repeated exchange of thoughts, ideas, and beliefs also facilitate relationships. A prime example is the Web, where people from all over (low physical propinquity) bond in chat rooms, forums, and online communities.

If you don't have a blog or a Facebook presence, create one now. Posts are your way to expose others to who you are; responding is the others' way to do the same. Being online can never replace personal presence, but engaging in cyberspace nonetheless mirrors how we get to know people in the real world.

The figure below pictures the sharp contrasts between someone simply knowing who you are (a name, a face) and someone getting to know who you are (your thoughts, hopes, and dreams).

Aware	Know	Like	Trust
Least profitable		More Profitable	
Run marketing campaigns		Build relationships	
Constant grind		Enjoyable and fun	
Have a job		Own a business	
Not sustainable		Sustainable	

No matter the medium, the more we interact with people we know, the more we tend to like them and vice versa. Sincerity is what leads to trust and influence as well as repeat and referral business – which is the foundation and fuel for a sustainable business.

WHY IS
THE POINT

"The interesting thing is: if you do it for love,
the money comes anyway."
– Richard St. John

If you have your own children, have nieces or nephews, or have
been around kids for any amount of time, you know that one of
kids' favorite words is why. "Why is the sky blue?" "Why is that
woman in a wheelchair?" "Why do goldfish die?" According to a
recent study, children ask such questions (and so many of them)
to get to the truth. In fact, children typically persist in their line
of questioning (or invent an alternate interpretation) when an
answer is unfulfilling. On the other hand, when given a clear and
direct explanation, children are satisfied or move on to yet another
question.

Adults ask why just as often as children, if not more, but we aren't as
conscious of it. Adults can also be lazy and quit or capitulate rather
than pursue a line of questioning. (Adults do this in relationships,
at work, and in introspection.) Adults take shortcuts, too, or mimic
what appears to be successful.

Many companies in the real estate industry proffer shortcuts. There is certainly plenty of demand, and suppliers are happy to oblige. Thus, there is no end of seminars, tools, and techniques available for sale.

The truth is, just because a process works for one agent, there's no guarantee you can recreate its success. Two agents can seemingly work alike in the same market in the same number of hours and the outcomes can and likely will be wholly different. Why? Success can't be attributed to a process; success is tied to a person.

There are essentially two ways to influence human behavior: You can *manipulate* it or you can *inspire* it.

Here, manipulate doesn't refer to subversive, deceptive, or unethical practices. For example, if you manipulate your commission rate low enough, you may cause people to do business with you. Other examples of manipulation include "flat fee" and "MLS only" pricing, or, if you're a broker, throwing a pizza party in the office to try to correct low morale.

The other way is to influence behavior is to inspire it. With this method, people take action because they want to. It feels right in their gut. For instance, one agent may engender trust by being true to her word. Another may enjoy repeat business because he is active in the community in which he lives and lists. Oversimplified, inspiration changes people.

Many agents and brokers struggle to influence clients. Collateral. Pricing. Marketing. Advertising. Social media. You can spend a lot of money in each category. Manipulation does not work. It's a shortcut and a salve.

What about inspiration? Few consider it. It's nebulous; there's no 20-point plan readily available to buy as an audiobook; and it requires a greater investment than a few hundred dollars. However, it provides a greater return over a long period of time.

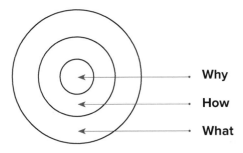

Simon Sinek is a teacher and speaker, credited with discovering the Golden Circle, which "explains why we are inspired by some people, leaders, messages, and organizations over others." According to Sinek there are two methods for businesses to communicate.

1. Communicate what you do and then talk about how you do it.

2. Communicate why you do it, then how you do it, and finally, what you do.

The first technique is by far the most common; in the real estate business, it's almost ubiquitous. A typical agent or broker starts with what he or she wants to do and then formulates how to achieve the goal. For example:

> What: "I want to make money."
> How: "I'll help people buy and sell homes."
> Why: "Uh. I want to make money."

If you lead with what you do, you're trying to make a sale armed solely with facts and figures and tactics. You may be equipped to manipulate the consumer into a transaction, but there's little chance of repeat business, raves, or referrals. Your business is beholden to advertising, marketing, and the constant demand to bring in new business — the most ineffective and unprofitable way to run a small business. I call it the "hamster wheel" — running and running, but making no forward progress. I ran on it for years.

Contrast the latter with a purposeful approach, exemplified by Yasu's email to me. Within five hours of meeting him, I knew how he came to live in Denver, how he and his brothers built a very successful business, and how much charitable endeavors meant to him personally. Yasu could have sent me a coupon to sell me more sushi, but instead he sold me on Yasu.

When you lead with "why," you reveal something about yourself and inspire others to reciprocate.

Your business is built on you.

Why should anyone care? The truth is, people don't buy *what* you do, they buy *why* you do it.

We're wired to be connected

We also see this in nature. It's how we're biologically wired. If you look at imagery of the human brain from the top down, you'll see it's broken down into three major components that correlate perfectly with the Golden Circle.

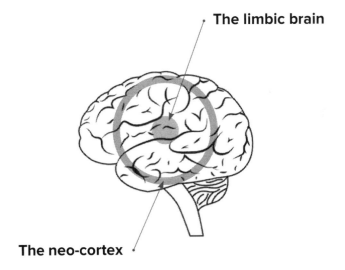

The limbic brain

The neo-cortex

The *neo-cortex* is responsible for all of our rational and analytical thought. When speaking to a home buyer about price per square foot, you're speaking to this part of the brain. You can give facts and figures until you are blue in the face, but if it just doesn't 'feel' right, or does not compute as rational, the sale is not going to happen.

The *limbic brain is* responsible for all of our feelings like trust and loyalty. It is also responsible for all our human behavior, all decision making, and has no capacity for language.

If *you* don't know what you do and why you do it, how will you ever get someone to identify with it, use your services, and more importantly, be loyal and refer their friends and family? It's not the more you give, the more you get. It's the more you give, the more you inspire others to give.

When you put yourself out there, when you take the risk based on time and energy, you inspire others to emulate that behavior, not for some kumbaya reason—it's just the anthropology of it. It strikes a chord with our inherent humanity and the core of our culture.

Prepare for some heavy lifting. We can't do it for you. But we'll give you a hint. A person may buy five to seven homes over the course of their lifetime. There is a lot of "life" going on in those 20-, 30-, or 40-year periods when they are *not* buying. Nonetheless, you can provide regular and considerable value to that relationship: inspire and help others and be genuine. Remember, this is all about people.

QUANTIFIED PORTFOLIO

The hard-nosed reality of real estate: Competition is fierce, choices are endless, and the cost of entry is negligible. Agents who build lasting relationships one by one by one will succeed in the new era. If the technical components are the craft, relationships are the art.

If you're looking for a quick path to real estate stardom or doing 40 deals in the next 90 days—we don't want to disappoint or blow smoke up your rear—this is not what this book is about.

We've been very clear, that to approach your real estate business with tactics, marketing schemes, the latest social networking craze, or the next big internet fad – isn't a recipe for sustainability. We've said from the first chapter, that for this to work (and it will), you're going have to work hard, be dedicated, work when you don't want to, continually improve as a human being, offer value in life (more than just real estate services), and plan on sticking with the right daily habits for at least three years before you have an actual *business*— as opposed to owning a job that you're scrambling at month after month, year after year.

We've learned that there is no guarantee that growth for growth's sake will make a difference in your business. You can have more agents on your team, more direct-mail going out, more emails being sent, and no one actually buying. You can have more traffic to your website, and only crickets on your phone lines.

There is a big difference between meaningful and hollow growth. The difference is depth, connection to your 'why,' and people.

For the wonderful opportunities that lie within our industry, we sure do have a tough business. Traditional "long tail" business rules don't easily apply to us. We typically have one product (service) to sell. Our customers buy from us every seven years, and most agents don't put in the work to build a deep relationship with them.

Other than being in a perpetual state of prospecting, marketing, advertising, and otherwise begging for business, what can an agent do to escape the missing long tail of the real estate business?

Stop Shouting and LISTEN

The most valuable asset of any successful small business, whether it be a garage, a salon, or a real estate brokerage, is its regular clientele. Whether it's the diner who eats lunch twice a week at the same lunch counter or the homeowner who calls Moe's Plumbing whenever a clog develops, repeat customers provide a steady return and a base to expand upon.

But the word clientele is rather antiseptic. I prefer to call the people you're most connected to your "portfolio." In fact, that moniker is apropos, because like a collection of stocks or real estate holdings, investing in your people portfolio returns dividends. Approach each relationship with authenticity and it's yours to keep for life no matter where your career and passions take you.

Your objective is to build a portfolio of one thousand people. A portfolio of that size can generate approximately sixty to one hundred and twenty transactions a year, reliably, in nearly any market conditions. It is the only path to a sustainable real estate business, and it can't be faked. If your daily activities revolve around meeting new people and building rewarding relationships, in about three years, you'll have a substantive portfolio and a healthy business.

While we recommend a goal of a thousand people, the ultimate size of your portfolio is entirely up to you. As you can see from the following chart, even five hundred people in your portfolio can produce a robust, sustainable business.

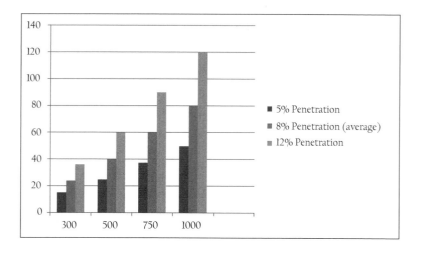

You can't take shortcuts with this. You can't build a portfolio from a mailing list. Knocking on doors alone won't do it nor will mass emails. Building your portfolio is more like farming than hunting. Curating a people portfolio requires emotion, mindfulness, and energy. You must invest yourself.

So, who qualifies as a member of your portfolio? Anyone who:

- Loves what you do. The person understands your 'why', knows about your life, your family, your favorite things, your community connections, and your hobbies.
- Engages. If you reach out to the person (via phone, text, email, or Facebook), you'll eventually hear back.
- Relates. You can have a comfortable lunch with the person. I'm not mandating you have to have lunch with each person

in your portfolio— although you should try. I'm saying you would genuinely enjoy each other's company.

In short, your portfolio is full of people that want to be associated with you, stay in touch with you, and advocate for you. When anyone in your portfolio thinks about real estate, he or she thinks of you and sings your praises to others.

Of course, not everyone you meet is going to become a part of your portfolio. Not everyone is going to engage and relate. And that's okay. Stay in contact with them anyway. Write down every name and contact information you receive and stay in touch.

So how do you ensure that you don't just collect a bunch of lukewarm dabblers? How do you find people that are willing to take up arms for your cause, that will vehemently support your work and connect with your 'why'?

There are two keys: Relevance and positive context. To gain members into your People Portfolio, you must be and remain highly relevant. Your work in real estate isn't enough (that's a baseline requirement). People need to identify with you as a human being and see you engaged in community and growth.

So now you know what you do, "why" you do it, and how many people you need to have a sustainable business, but how do you find these people. How do you attract them?

ATTRACTION

There are two types of agents: *personality agents* and *process agents.*

Personality agents are those with the "larger than life" personalities that can instantly charm others and are successful *because* of their personality—former professional sports players, strong personality salesman/saleswoman types, and other really outgoing people. This is the type of agent you see on real estate television shows. These types of agents are generally born this way and are not teachable.

Process agents are everyone else.

Most of us don't have that magical personality gift. I certainly don't, and truth be told, I'm even somewhat introverted. But that doesn't mean I can't attract people into my portfolio or that I don't deserve to. One lesson life has taught me is that everyone matters, no matter who they are or what they do.

Yes, I mean you, too!

Yasu from Sushi Den boils down his success to a single word: trust. People trust that the experience they get night after night will be stellar. His clientele trusts that they will receive the highest quality food and service.

Authenticity is a rare commodity these days. People gravitate to genuineness when they see it, and more importantly when they feel it. If enough people hear about the things you do, the kind of person you are, the dreams you dream, and the hopes that keep you plugging away towards your goal, you'll attract plenty of people into your portfolio!

Yasu's community activism goes far beyond contributing money to charitable causes. Some restaurant locations serve as the anchor of neighborhood renewals, attracting other businesses and residents to what might otherwise become blight.

Give your portfolio as much free value as you can—and I'm not talking about calendars, pens, or magnets. Here are some suggestions.

- Sponsor free community workshops. Introduce your portfolio to the best health and wealth practitioners you can find.

- Organize a local farmer's market or a community garden.

- Organize micro-events for your town, such as inviting authors, professors, scientists, and technology experts.

You can do a lot more than you realize. So, you deserve 1,000 people in your portfolio but how do you get them? Where do you find them? What do you do to attract them into your circle? In a word, you must be *remarkable*.

The word remarkable is confusing and is misinterpreted by many to be something far beyond what it really means. Seth Godin's best-selling book "Purple Cow" explains it nicely.

"When I say remarkable, I mean just that... It's worth talking about."

That's it. *Worth talking about.* That's remarkable! And it's not as insurmountable as we make it out to be in our heads. You, me, and others can be remarkable because we all can do things worth talking about. Knowing that, consider this old precept:

"Advertising is the tax you pay for NOT being remarkable."

When you think about it, you'll realize just how true that adage is. Advertising and marketing is the attempt of a business (or an individual) to try and stand out from the crowd, get noticed, and move the target audience to talk about them. In other words, advertising is an attempt to buy "remarkable."

It's cheaper *and easier* to be remarkable!

REAL
MARKABLE

"The place to improve the world is first in one's own heart and head and hands, and then work outward from there."
– Robert M. Pirsig

How can you be remarkable? Start with being REAL.

You can be remarkable in your business in many ways, just by being:

- The first – or last
- The cheapest – or priciest
- The easiest – or hardest
- The simplest – or most complex
- The highest – or lowest – value provider

The possibilities are limitless. Whatever it is you are doing now, there is a way to be remarkable at it by "upping your game," getting out of your comfort zone, and providing a unique experience.

Why Realvolve's portfolio thinks we're remarkable

There are dozens of technology providers in real estate. There are hundreds of coaches, writers, and authors, and millions of websites dedicated to real estate. But Realvolve stands out. We write books, have been in the real estate trenches, and are dedicated to changing agents' lives.

That alone may or may not qualify as remarkable, but here's is something that stands out: Realvolve is the only technology provider in real estate delving into issues beyond real estate, such as health, well-being, and sustainable business practices. Realvolve also donates proceeds from book sales to charity.

We don't see this as remarkable since we simply followed our hearts. As should you. What makes you remarkable may not feel worthy of a trophy—the trait or talent is likely inherent to who you are—but its expression will set you apart.

Being remarkable and attracting people to your "why" is a direct function of the actions you take and the proprietary contributions you provide to the world.

It's about becoming the kind of person that others look up to, draw inspiration and encouragement from, and want to emulate, follow, or support. Be that person, and your portfolio will naturally develop and grow. And chances are good that there will be far more than just 1,000 people in your portfolio!

One mile at a time

The path of creating portfolio of 1,000 is more of a *marathon* than a *sprint*. Most agents won't do it because it's laborious, time intensive, and results do not appeal to our culture's incessant need for instant gratification. But I'm guessing you're not most agents. I'm guessing you were brought here to do more than what's already been done. Be real, be you, be authentic and people will see and value the difference.

THE AUTHENTICITY PARADOX

*"The privilege of a lifetime
is to become who you truly are."*
— C.G. Jung

We, as small business owners, often get beckoned by that seducing siren of automated marketing, and any technology that promises quick results or boosted productivity, lead generating tactics at the hands of a machine doing the heavy lifting.

It's our nature. We like shortcuts. The path of least resistance describes the physical or metaphorical pathway that provides the least resistance to forward motion by a given object or entity, among a set of alternative paths.

So if your sole goal is to simply make a profit, go study the intricacies of Internet marketing and reduce your commissions and call it a day – but it won't last. It's not authentic.

Don't misunderstand; we're not saying that lead generation isn't important, it absolutely is. But if you can't grasp the fundamental difference between an action to generate a lead versus an activity to build a relationship with a human being - you may as well quit and go start an ant farm, because this isn't going to work out long term for you.

If your goal is to build a real estate business that will make it past the 10-year anniversary mark and produce the means for you to live a great life, you can start by being authentic. Authenticity is not a tactic or strategy, it's about you. It's your 'why.' It's living within your purpose and passion – not because you were TOLD to operate this way to be more profitable, but because you NEED and WANT to, it's coming from inside of you because it's right.

Traditional marketing tactics (open houses, email blasts, online marketing, social media, etc.) done solely for the sake of attention can work to produce sales, and you're going to need to do them in the beginning, but they are far less likely to lead to relationships that matter to your people portfolio.

Then there is "salesmanship." I am not a fan of practiced scripts that feel forced. Scripts are robotic, fall short of being authentic, and feel wrong. Scripts exist only to manipulate a sale.

Add value to the community you serve. Give back. Don't just extract money. Agents who give back to their communities not only build better businesses, they lead healthier, more fulfilling lives.

Many wise observers of human life have taught different versions of generosity. An ancient Hebrew proverb states, "One man gives freely, yet gains even more; another withholds unduly, but ends up impoverished."

The Buddha taught that "Giving brings happiness at every stage of its expression." A Hindu proverb holds that "They who give have all things, they who withhold have nothing." And Jesus said, "Whoever tries to keep his life will lose it, and whoever loses his life will preserve it."

The trick, though, is that you cannot use generosity as a tactic or strategy. It can't be faked to achieve some self-serving end. If you give your energy to your community, it will give back to you.

THE VALUE OF LISTENING

"A wise old owl lived in an oak,
The more he saw the less he spoke.
The less he spoke the more he heard.
Why can't we all be like that wise old bird?
– unknown

Conventional wisdom would say that real estate is no place for shyness. We're trained to ask probing questions, be prepared with follow-up responses, and we usually end up with much more output than input. All in an effort to avoid that painful word: No.

We avoid that word. It hurts. Evolution has programmed us to feel rejection in our guts. This is how the tribe enforced obedience, by wielding the threat of expulsion. Fear of rejection isn't just psychological; it's biological. It's in our cells.

So for me, early in my career, the act of cold-calling and knocking on doors was not only unpleasant – it was like fighting with myself at a molecular level.

To add to that, I'm from Arizona – not exactly known as one of the more outgoing places. People are polite and nice, but I believe due to the nomadic nature of the state, most keep to themselves. So when my family moved to Colorado and we took our first walk through the neighborhood and someone said, "Hi, how are you doing? Any plans this weekend?" I looked at my kids and said under my breath, "Why is she talking to us?"

To tap an old cliché, "We have one mouth and two ears for a reason."

An important developmental milestone is the ability to speak. However, *listening* is an equally if not more important skill that is often overlooked by parents, educators, and, of course, zealous real estate trainers.

Certainly, we are taught to listen (mind) to our parents and to listen in school. However, few of us are taught the active, disciplined skill to examine the information we hear rather than picking up 'clues' to formulate a response or think of our own goals while someone else talks. Active listening improves the quality and quantity of information we comprehend, and thereby improves our decision making.

Bernard Ferrari, author of *Power Listening: Mastering the Most Critical Business Skill of All*, states that good listening is the key to developing fresh insights and ideas that fuel success.

"The most basic and powerful way to connect to another person is to listen. Just listen. Perhaps the most important thing we ever give each other is our attention…. A loving silence often has far more power to heal and to connect than the most well-intentioned words. " - Rachel Naomi Remen

Look at the average agent in our industry. A typical agent spends 80-90% of their precious time chasing clients, conducting marketing, talking about themselves, pushing services, and sending mass canned email. Perhaps agents should be listening?

We live in wonderful times. People are sharing their lives on social media. Thanks to sites like Linkedin, Facebook, Twitter, we can folllow their lives as they unfold. If we listen, they'll tell us:

- When their kids win a sports game
- When they change jobs or get a promotion
- What their favorite foods are

Changing the way we have conversations with people is not an easy feat to accomplish and change is hard, but it's the foundation of where connections are built.

CHASE THE PASSION - NOT THE MONEY

"I had decided to stop chasing the money, and start chasing the passion."

— Tony Hsieh, Founder of Zappos

When I started in real estate, mandated office meetings were the norm. I worked in the area's busiest real estate company and our meetings routinely had 100+ agents in attendance. The backdrop of these meetings was the sales leader board.

I'm reasonably well versed in the psychology of 'social proof,' and I'm not going to judge whether that practice is good or bad – but it is true that it has an affect on our brains, our nature, and our emotions.

It's natural to compare ourselves to others and often unavoidable. Unfortunately, because we can only compare the things that we can objectively measure, we live in a world that is obsessed with measuring and comparing externals. Somewhere along the way, we decided that we could determine who is living a more valuable life by comparing their cars, computers and the number of transactions on a sales board.

Simply put, we tied self-worth to net-worth. As a painful result, we begin to rate our happiness and our mental well-being based on these externals – that are only as real as someone's monthly production.

Real estate, indeed life, is a mental game. The search for happiness is universal. People from all corners and in all sorts of circumstances seek this elusive thing called happiness. Isn't that what you are seeking? Isn't that why you're reading this book?

Happiness is a goal for nearly all of us. But there are different ideas floating around about what exactly makes people happy. Is money the key to happiness? It's been studied and determined that, for people who are struggling to provide for their basic needs (food, clothing, shelter), more money can make them happier, but only up to a certain point.

When a person is able to provide for themselves and their families at a basic but comfortable level, more money doesn't increase their happiness. So, if you earn $75,000 a year, earning $300,000 a year isn't going to make you happier.

A recent study found that while life evaluation rose steadily with annual income, the quality of the respondents' everyday experiences did not improve beyond approximately $75,000 a year[1].

In another study by Zappos[2], happiness was the total of four main elements:

1. Perceived Control
2. Perceived Progress
3. Connectedness (number and depth of your relationships)
4. Vision/Meaning (being part of something bigger than yourself)

Those are four powerful cornerstones. Strive to separate what you can and cannot control. Give yourself credit where credit is due. Build lasting bonds. Become part of something bigger. Let these mantras guide the progress and development of your business. It's not about the money. It's about the people.

Commit to the craft. Know your "why." Serve your community. Build a people portfolio. And do it all with passion.

Endnotes

[1] Study performed by Princeton University http://wws.princeton.edu/news/Income_Happiness/

[2] Study performed by Zappos http://www.deliveringhappiness.com/

US

"Alone we can do so little;
together we can do so much."

— **Helen Keller**

LETTERS
FROM LEADERS

When I set out to write this book , I quickly found that I was just scratching the surface and needed to reach beyond my own experience if I was to provide a true depth of value to you and the industry.

In the process, *Part II* of *REAL* ended up not only bridging the gaps, but offers what I feel is the most diverse collection of thinking and wisdom in our industry. The contributions have created one of the deepest, most complete books ever written on what it takes to sustainably succeed in real estate, from philosophic values, to business fundamentals.

I am deeply grateful and humbled to have collaborated with these leaders. The amount of thought and care each person poured into his or her chapter is reflected in the honest nature of each and every word, and I am honored that so many were willing to bare it all in hopes of contributing to the shift toward artisanship in real estate.

And after reading all of the submissions, a funny thing happened. What once felt like an industry of competitors transformed into a community of collaborators and innovators. Indeed, each of us has a responsibility to contribute our gifts to the greater good of our industry. It's clear now that it is about us. We're all in this together.

SUCCESS IS PUTTING PEOPLE FIRST

Austin Allison
CEO, dotloop
@gaustinallison

I was introduced to real estate when I bought my first house—a small fixer-upper just outside of Cincinnati—at age 17. A result of many pennies saved up over the years, the purchase was not only a big milestone, but also a turning point in my life.

I distinctly remember being shocked by all of the paper involved in the process. My father owned a small construction company and my mother was in information technology. With that background, I was naturally ecstatic to be a homeowner, yet frustrated by the stressful experience leading up to closing the deal. It was the wet signatures, the late-night faxes, the piles of paperwork and documentation, etc. There had to be a better way to do business.

So much more than a numbers game

Despite a transaction experience inconsistent with my expectations, I caught the real estate bug and decided to pursue it in college, confident that a few hours of effort each week would result in bigger commissions than I could count. How wrong I was!

I sold real estate through college and quickly began to see the realities of being a real estate agent while juggling life, education and a career. It was tiresome to say the least. Between racing from class to get to a showing, signing documents on the hood of my car and communicating through multiple means of technology, I was inspired to create dotloop. And though my role in real estate has changed quite a bit over the years, the lessons I learned as an agent (and a consumer) about the importance of relating on a human level is something we've incorporated into how we've built the company. It's also a major reason why we've been so successful.

One of those lessons is that selling real estate is so much more than a numbers game. It's hard work and involves more roles than merely that of an agent in a transaction: you're a strategist in helping a client make their offer, a negotiator when the client gets locked in a bidding war and a counselor when a dream home goes off the market. Most importantly, you're the catalyst in the transaction process at large.

The truly successful real estate agents, a far smaller and more elite group than you may think, understand that success stems from a delicate balance of attention, compassion, positivity — and humanness. Agents who put people at the center of the equation are the ones who win big, now and in the future.

Put people first

Success in real estate is simple: Put people first and give them an enjoyable experience that's on their terms, not yours. This has always been the case, of course, but technology has made it easy to remove people from the process. We all are loyal to great experiences – be it personal attention sealed with a handshake or the ability to close a deal from 1,500 miles away.

Real estate is an industry that revolves around people. Buying a home is a big decision with strong emotional and financial factors involved. A cumbersome transaction process will only add to the stress of that experience. It's your role to minimize those bad feelings and make sure it's an enjoyable experience.

At dotloop, we call it Peoplework. It's a belief about putting people first and giving clients the sort of experience you'd hope to receive while making a decision as big as buying a home. You would never want to be treated as just a number – and neither do your clients.

In any industry – real estate included – setting out to make the most money by working with as many clients as possible is a recipe for disaster. Instead, I've learned that delivering a positive experience to a smaller list of clients actually pays higher dividends. Filling the funnel the right way is the best thing you can do to build a sustainable business.

People are Loyal to Great Experiences

People are loyal to great experiences. While that's not a new or novel concept, what is new is truly making it happen in your own business – and leveraging inspiration from companies in other industries that do this well every day.

Starbucks, for example, knows that you can buy coffee anywhere, but if they provide the consistent experience you want from a coffee shop (a barista who remembers your name and order, free WiFi, comfortable couches and no pressure to leave), you'll come back every time your caffeine withdrawals kick in.

Or, consider Apple. They have reinvented the brick and mortar retail experience, allowing you to experiment with their technology hands-on before making a purchase. The Apple Store gives you a blank slate to create the experience you want, whether it's the opportunity to ask hundreds questions or the ease of just handing over your credit card to pay immediately. You leave feeling satisfied, and in return, Apple can expect that you'll come back to purchase from them again.

Real Estate Is No Different

Real estate is no different. Invest in customer service as marketing – rather than traditional marketing. Lead with processes and operational excellence before direct marketing and lead generation. Go out of your way to make every experience enjoyable and memorable. Buyers and sellers can work with any agent in your market – some are even choosing not to use an agent at all – but if you create a name for yourself as an agent who delivers the best experience in town, you'll have customers for life.

If you create a well-executed, thoughtful experience, you'll leave a memorable impression. And in doing so, you'll see more business than you could ever get from direct marketing, SEO, ad-words or social media and prime real estate on consumer listing portals combined. Like Apple and Starbucks – and many other companies across all industries – have demonstrated, putting your customers' experience front and center is what separates the successful from those that are just spinning their wheels.

WHEN PASSION
AND BUSINESS
COLLIDE

Lisa Archer

Co-founder, Geeky Girls

@lisaarcher

I joined the banking industry right out of college. I loved the work and became very successful, readily eclipsing my sales goals. However, the rigors of a 9-to-5 job and an hour-long commute to and from the office took a toll on my family. In 2006, with my daughter just a year old, I resigned my position at the bank to get a real estate license.

Good decision, terrible timing, as the market crashed shortly after I obtained licensure. At that point, in something of a whole new world, every sale was grueling. It took longer and longer to sell a property; securing a mortgage was near impossible; and each appraisal seemed like a pull on a one-armed bandit. Needless to say, stress was the only constant, and by the fall of 2010, I was burning out. It was time again to stop and reconsider. I desperately needed a change of scenery. I wanted to do things differently. I wanted independence.

After a move in 2011 from Texas to Charlotte, North Carolina, I enlisted my dad as partner and started an intense mission to build an independent brokerage. He and I hired three buyer partners in four months and have never looked back. We ended 2012 rebranding our team "Live Love Charlotte." We also partnered with Laurie Davis to create Live Love, Inc., which now includes an extension "Live Love Pinehurst" [Pinehurst, North Carolina is a resort city best known for its challenging golf courses.] and an investor division. At last count, the firm employs twenty-seven people, including agents and staff. As I write this, we hope to expand into two additional North Carolina metropolitan areas.

One of the biggest passions of Live Love, Inc. is social media. In 2012, Facebook surpassed one billion users — that's an enormous number and demonstrates the potential of the platform. But like communication via traditional outlets, your message must be crafted to fit the media. You wouldn't walk up to someone at a backyard BBQ and start spouting new listings, so why do the same on Facebook and Twitter?

Everyone knows I sells real estate, but no one hates to know it. This has been my mantra for several years. Generally, ninety percent of my posts are personal and only ten percent discuss business. Business is not my focus; relationships are.

If you've never had a referral via social media, reconsider and reformulate what you are doing. Are you listening? Can you see what's happening in others' lives? If no, set up a list and scan it daily for life events — births, promotions, weddings, birthdays — you should "Like" or comment on.

Mobile applications make it simple to stay engaged with little effort. You can now respond to an Twitter mention while you are waiting at a doctor's office or update your status from the line at the grocery store.

A word of caution, though. It's safe to say nothing is private anymore. You need to be careful about what you write because it's very difficult to rescind a post or tweet (as many politicians, pundits, and companies have learned the hard way).

Social Media is an amazing tool if you use it for what it was intended for. Listen to what others are saying and then do what any good friend would do. Once you have everyone on a list, follow along regularly and reinforce each connection. People like to do business with people they know, like and trust. Stay engaged and the referrals will follow.

BURN THIS BOOK

Matthew Beall

Broker, Hawaii Life Real Estate

@mattbeall

Here's a Zen koan.

An elderly Zen master lived in a remote village. The master had practiced Zen his entire life and his knowledge and wisdom was cherished by all who knew him.

On his deathbed, the master summoned his most accomplished acolyte and gave the apprentice a massive leather-bound book. Filled with handwritten passages, the master explained the book was his personal journal, containing insights he had amassed his entire life and all the secrets of Zen. The master explained that upon his death, the student would become the new master, and he advised the student to rely on the wisdom of the book for guidance and assistance.

When the master died, the student immediately burned the book.

I've worked in real estate for fifteen years. I've made billions of dollars of sales, I've managed hundreds of agents, and I'm here to tell you to suspect any advice I have to offer.

Why? Real estate is an industry of over a million people in the United States. It's both a massive and hugely varied industry, with markets that are wholly dissimilar. It's also very dynamic. The real estate industry constantly changes. Given such multiplicity and tumult, there's an extraordinary amount of advice available — but most of it is absolute hogwash.

Here's a personal anecdote. A friend of mine is a golf pro. He knew I had never played the game, so he gave me a free lesson one year for my birthday. The first thing he said to me, even before I picked up a club, was, "Don't listen to anyone." Or, as he elaborated, be warned every golfer has an opinion he or she is anxious to share. How to swing. What club to use. The proper grip. His sage advice: Ignore all of it. Instead, he recommended, learn one way and make adjustments to that original approach over time and with professional tutelage. It's brilliant advice, for golf and real estate.

I'm sure this book mentions at least a dozen times there's virtually no barrier to entry in real estate. As a result, the industry has its share of uneducated, get-rich-quick types, addicts of every kind, and unfortunately, a lot of total morons. (There, I said it.) Combine the motley crew with the cultural trend of instant-gratification (social media, text messaging, Google), and the result is an entire cottage industry that exists simply to sell things to real estate agents. Marketing. Software. Websites. Apps. Books. Collateral. Conferences. Media of every kind. And real estate agents eat it up, shelling out big bucks to buy the latest bright and shiny object, because so many want a shortcut to success. If this book isn't about how to build and maintain a real estate career that sustains itself, you should probably consider burning it. Seriously, if there's one bit of advice I can offer, it's to maintain a healthy skepticism of the "advice" given to real estate salespeople.

And with that out of the way, let's get on to more advice.

Listen

Stephen Covey, the notable management consultant and author, said, "Most people do not listen with the intent to understand; they listen with the intent to reply." Agreed. The truth is you don't know what you don't know. And you're new. Don't try to compensate by talking incessantly about what you do know. Instead, listen. Listen to your prospects. Listen to your brokers. Listen to cooperating agents. Ask them questions, and then really listen.

Learn to write

One of my top salespeople types using two index fingers. Yes, he is (very) slow, but he is also very effective. He only focuses on what matters, because he can't afford to ramble. He's concise. He gets to the point quickly. He gets results.

Sales and relationships revolve around conversations. In turn, conversations revolve around words. Words matter, as does diction. Whether conscious of it or not, people form impressions of you reading your diction and syntax. If you can write clear, readable, crisp email messages (still the leading generator of new leads), listings, market newsletters, and blog posts, you'll win.

Don't make assumptions

When I started my career, I sat open house a lot. I work in a resort market, so people from all over the country would come into my open houses. Often, they would ask the price of the listing, and then sound surprised afterwards. I learned to ask them, "Are you surprised because the price is higher or lower than you thought?" It's a great question, for so many reasons. Regardless of their answer, the question itself creates a context for the prospects. It tells them that there are people who might feel the opposite. It also gets them talking. Why are they surprised? What are they comparing it to?

In similar situations, I learned to rephrase the question "Where are you from?" because that question assumes the person is not local. I live and work in Hawaii, where people either strongly identify with already living here, or at the very least don't want it to be obvious that they don't live here. So, I changed the question to "Where is home for you?" or "Where is home for you now?" The latter question is apt because many attendees of an open house are considering a move. It also opens a dialog with prospective sellers. Many times, the visitors to an open house are neighbors, measuring what homes in the neighborhood are selling for. I learned not to alienate them asking "Where are you from?"

If you're going to kick ass, you have to take names

Another mistake new salespeople make is not taking names. You, the new real estate agent, are now in the business of people. Not properties, people. Properties will always be there. The people won't.

Take names. Record them. Track them. Take notes. Don't let them out of your sight. Use a system to keep track of the people you meet and follow up with each and every one. Whatever you do, don't allow any name go unrecorded. Contact information is the currency of your new business.

If you're going to work a specific neighborhood or market niche, learn the names and preferences of the owners. Who are they? Why do they live in the area? What makes them tick? What's your relationship to them? Of course, you have to know the commodity, too — the details of various properties and what makes each one valuable. But properties are not what your stock in trade. Relationships are.

Cooperate

Real estate is one of the only industries in the world that requires cooperation among competitors. Whether the competition works in the same brokerage as you or in a competing office, you have to get along with others to succeed in this business.

Don't let things fester. If you have a disagreement or issue with an agent, clear it up immediately. Save face. If the other agent is wrong, a jerk, or even outright insufferable, suck it up. Other brokers should hold you in very high regard.

You need others, and you always will. Even if a peer leaves the business, stay on good terms, since he or she could easily become a client. (I've sold a lot of real estate for people who used to be in the business.)

Tell them to "Fuck off!"

Strangely, this might be the best advice I've ever been given.

Very early in my career, I was working on my first sale over $1 million with a friendly, cooperative broker (who has since become a mentor of mine). The $1 million sale was all cash, with a 7-day close. It was short and simple, and the clients on both sides were very happy. At the same time, I had a client who was horribly litigious. He sued everyone, for everything, all the time. (I didn't learn about this until it was too late.) While the deal was small, it was unnecessarily complicated, with incessant bickering over tiny details, countless threats, and a raft of lawyers.

While lamenting the souring deal to the cooperating broker in my big sale, he said, "You know, Matt, sometimes you have to tell them to fuck off!" I was shocked, not because of his language, but at the very idea. I actually had the thought "You can do that?" Indeed you can and should. Even if you are in survival mode, needing every dollar, as I did, you have to realize there are costs involved in taking on business that's personally compromising.

You don't have to work with everybody. You can pick and choose. It's a radical thing to consider, especially when you're just starting out and don't have any business, but you can set boundaries with prospects. And when you do, it works.

Get a coach

After about 12 years in the business, I finally hired a business coach. I feel like I wasted 12 years.

One of the first things I learned from my business coach was how to hire. The real estate business isn't getting any easier. You can't do it all, and even if you could, you can't grow a business to any scale going solo.

The classic mistake most salespeople make (myself included), is that they prospect like mad, garner a bunch of business, and then get totally bogged down trying to close that business — ironically leaving no time for prospecting. It's boom or bust in a vicious cycle. Worse, most salespeople call for help when already overwhelmed. It's a recipe for disaster. Hiring under duress favors convenience not correctness. Whether help comes in the form of an assistant, another agent, or both, hiring right requires patience, practice, and discipline.

Hiring right also requires a good dose of humility. Know your weaknesses and hire to offset your personal shortcomings. For example, I'm a self-starter and tend to rebel against authority. I don't like being told what to do. While admirable in some ways, my psychological disposition is nonetheless a liability. My hires — and my coach — provide corrections. In fact, I've found that agents who work with a coach do far better in their careers.

Don't think that you can't afford a coach. The truth is that you can't afford not to hire a coach. And don't just pick anybody. Get a pro. Find a coach that has a proven track record.

And burn this book.

INGREDIENTS FOR SUCCESS IN REAL ESTATE

Vanessa Bergmark

Partner, Red Oak Realty

@vbredoak

Picture this: It's 2001. The place is the [San Francisco] Bay Area. The economy is booming, dotcoms occupy every nook and cranny, and the only thing inflating faster than the Internet bubble is the price of homes. From Berkeley to Saratoga, demand far exceeds supply. It's a seller's market. Multiple bids, outright bidding wars, and overbids are commonplace. For even the most stalwart buyer, house hunting is exasperating. But I loved it.

Mind you, I wasn't a realtor at the time. I was a buyer, and the experience was vexatious. My husband and I spent almost a year casting and losing bids on one house after another. Yet even when the phone rang with crushing news of yet another failed offer — "You came in eighth," or "Two other offers were higher" — I was hooked. Moreover, I was fascinated.

So, with my own home finally purchased, I quit my day job, negotiated a one-year pass with my husband, and started a real estate career. I expected little, if any, income in the first twelve months, but I was determined to succeed, or perhaps driven to not become an employee again.

At first, the freedom is delicious. It's very liberating to wake without an alarm, stay in pajamas, and enjoy a third cup of coffee before setting down to work. And there's the rub: What is work when your sofa is your office? There's no product to create. No one looks over your shoulder; and deadlines and accountability are self-imposed. How do you spend the day, let alone craft a career? To many, the lack of structure is anathema. Frankly, how you behave as your own boss largely determines whether you succeed or fail.

Some ten years into my real estate career, and now an owner of a brokerage with eighty sales people, I'd like to share some ingredients for success.

Treat your work like a job

We joke in the industry about the low barrier of entry into real estate: Taking a real estate course is a nominal expense, and passing an exam is the only hurdle to launching a career as an agent. But licensure is really the easiest task you'll ever face. If you want a productive, sustainable career in real estate, you have to take the work seriously. Building your business takes time, patience, focus, energy, and money.

Let me rephrase that: Running your business takes time, patience, focus, energy, and money. On your first day and on every day thereafter, you must always be learning. Educate yourself not only on trends, legal contracts, and local nuances, but the challenges and market forces that confront consumers. Don't treat your role as a part-time job. Clients expect and deserve a realtor that' expertly informed.

Create a business plan

Of course, like running any business, you can use tools to organize, track your schedule, and stay connected. But more important, create your own business plan.

When I joined my first agency, the broker asked me to create a budget and a business plan. I was also told to write down the exact amount I wanted to earn that year. Huh? Proofing a contract and opening a lockbox seemed more immediate, relevant, and tangible pursuits, but I assembled the plan all the same. I wrote down a number. A healthy number.

Some eighteen months later (around the time I did my taxes) I realized just how much such a seemingly inconsequential exercise had influenced my results. I exceeded my already aggressive target by $10,000. Writing that plan, making goals concrete, helped me identify and stratify my priorities. To this day, on each anniversary, I still write down a number. Sure, completing a fill-in-the-box business plan may seem hokey at first, but do it anyway. The process forces you to think about what you actually need to do.

Organize a formal schedule, too. It too may start somewhat contrived, but establishing a routine is a necessity in this business. Your schedule is your virtual boss. Time-block your lead generation schedule. Be certain to schedule brokerage meetings, training, and one-on-one coaching with your broker or mentor. Put your dates on a calendar to help acquaint yourself with the inventory, neighborhoods, and other players in the business.

Block out time for your own education, and yes, make time for life, too. As your career evolves, what you invest your time on will change, as will your goals, but you should always have a plan.

Understand the business, but understand the people, too

Real estate is about sales, but it's about relationships first. The most effective agents focus on people.

The Golden Rule may be cliche, but that doesn't diminish its truth. From clients and colleagues, to vendors and competitors, be fair, be intelligent, and be respectful. I like to say that each escrow is akin to the tango: move with confidence, but try not to step on your partner's feet. If a client feels cared for, she'll be far more likely to refer you to others. If an agent feels you were fair and honorable, he'll be more receptive to your next offer, share information with you, and look for new opportunities to work together.

The truth about lead generation. Truth be told, the best real estate agents usually don't turn paperwork in on time, show up promptly at the office every morning, or even advertise widely. Instead, the best are usually not working.

Soon after I started my career in real estate, I realized that attending a barbecue with strangers or celebrating Christmas with my neighborhood was actually part of my job. Each was a chance to connect, put myself out there, and create and further relationships.

Yes, you have to generate leads, but there are plenty of opportunities to do it and have fun. You can volunteer, chair a community group, or promote a charitable cause, all the while developing clientele.

Value your family, your health, and your downtime

Now you have established goals, a regular schedule, and your days are filled engaging with people. Your career has taken off and you are successful. Congratulations. Now here's the trick: You have to stay successful in life as well.

Virtually all the advice so far can be applied to your personal and family life just as well. Find the time to work out, rock climb, bike ride, or do yoga or crossfit. Find activities that challenge you. Take a vacation every year at a minimum. Schedule time off to take stock of your success or just to recharge. Turn off your phone and laptop and engage with your partner, your kids, and your soul.

If asked to name the trait that's most valuable in this business, I'd say *tenacity*. It's getting up every day, doing the job over and over again, all the while striving to do better. When the market shifts, you adjust and don't go out of business. When you get tired or frustrated, you remain engaged, get over the hurdle, and re-focus.

Doggedness makes all the difference.

CHANGE OR
BE CHANGED!

Kim Colaprete
Founder, Team Diva Real Estate Partners
@seattledivas

I decided in 1999 to leave my career in the non-profit activist world and join the glamorous world of real estate. At the time, real estate seemed very glam compared to HIV/AIDS community organizing. I was so disillusioned with the non-profit world and so desperate for a major change in my life that anything would have been better. Plus, I was ready to make some money!

Even before HGTV, I bought into the myth that real estate would be an easy way to make big bucks without having to work so hard. I wanted a "get out of job, get out of debt" free card and I thought real estate was the solution: no boss, no clocking in, no one controlling how much I could or could not earn. To me, real estate was a dream job, but ultimately my preconceived notions were without a clue. Although I chose my new career in real estate for all the wrong reasons, in the end, it was one of the best decisions I ever made.

So, shaved-headed lifelong activist me, who had never worked in any type of corporate environment or without a steady paycheck, decided to high dive head first into my new profession.

My first year of real estate was brutal. I did manage to close few deals quickly, but I spent months feeling like I was just a floundering mess. Even though I was closing deals, the money was pouring out faster than it was coming in. But, by then it was too late to quit; I was in it to win it and there was no place else to go, so this girl just had to make it work! And work I did. I would drive anywhere, meet with anyone, and work through the most difficult and tedious process just to get the deal done and make my clients happy. Far from the glamorous life I envisioned, but I was having a ton of fun, meeting great folks, and laying the foundations of a solid business.

After a few years, I became what many folks would call a "good" agent: your solid bread-and-butter, 15-20 deals a year agent. I was well liked by my clients and was well respected by my colleagues, but I was not yet at "top agent" strata. Bottom line, I had not gotten into this business just to settle for "good," so I kept working.

Then came 2008. Change. Massive, unplanned, uncontrolled, unrelenting change was upon us. Just months before the first bank went belly up, my assistant decided to go back to school, and my partner Chavi, decided on a whim to quit her job at Starbucks and come join me in this crazy profession.

The first couple of months of Chavi working with me were nuts. Although I was ecstatic to have her at the office with me, it was like Madonna asking Lady Gaga to come on tour and then expecting her to sing back up. We did not know how to work with each other, which added some unplanned chaos to our lives. To top it off, there was no more steady income from Chavi's stable corporate job. We were both accustomed to being "the divas" of our own organization. I was used to being large and in charge and so was she; now we had to learn to be large and in charge together. This change rattled my world. I could no longer be Ms. Real Estate Diva because now there was more than one Diva at the helm.

The fall of 2008 was a game changer for us gals and the Diva brand. We started to figure out how to work to each other's strengths. We had a practical problem as well as a personal problem—make up Chavi's lost Starbuck's income all while attempting to create a new business together as a real life power couple. Unbeknownst to us at that time, those problems and challenges were the impetus for discovering a novel way of doing business in real estate. Basically, we mixed in the power of my solid base of original Diva clients and fans with my obsession for visually stimulating marketing, and then added Chavi's creative project management skills for the perfect formula. The result was a whole new way of looking at our community and our business. Recession be damned!

The two of us started to gather a team of creative friends and business folks around us to develop a new and authentic Diva brand. We also started using social media as a way of connecting with our people and created strong messaging, which created a light at the end of the recession that we were going to reach. Maybe we could not control the economy, the market or consumer confidence but we could control our branding, our business practices, our marketing, and our attitude. So we started over. New economy + new world = new business.

Looking back I realize that Chavi's decision to leave corporate life and join me was our saving grace. Sure, we were broke for months and had to make the hard decision to invest most of our savings and earnings right back into developing what is now a thriving brand. At the time it was extremely scary and there were moments that we both questioned if this was the right path for us. However, every time we joined forces with one of our small business pals to host an event or throw a party, we opened the door to meeting a whole new crop of folks, many who are now part of the client, friend, and fan base that we call our Diva Divotees and Diva Dwellers. It is always in these moments of making these connections that we affirmed we were making the right decision.

This was my big recession lesson: change is not a business killer but a success maker. There is no easy pre-defined path to success. There are no tricks, no gimmicks, and no "if you do this for 99 days you will get 99 referrals." The reality is you have to be willing to go on instinct and sometimes fail. You have to test the waters and be open to going beyond those imagined boundaries that hinder our imagination and ideas.

For instance, the way Team Diva achieved star Yelp! status was by pure accident. We were at an open house and met a lovely young fella who was curious about green builders. We had a great chat and provided a ton of information. Later that week he came back to us and told us that he could not find us anywhere on the Web. At that point – we had a website but not much else. He recommended we start a Yelp! profile, so we did and, as it turned out, some of our best clients are also Yelpers, who gladly jump to leave us reviews. Now Yelp! is a huge lead generator for us.

The key lesson I've learned these past few years is that there is no set path to success in real estate. There is no *Binder to Real Estate, 8 Simple Rules of Success,* or *My iPad Made Me Millions* that is going to make you successful. The way to success is old-fashioned hard work, coupled with making mistakes, and the resilience to forge ahead. The tools you use may be the same as others in the business, but the way you build your own Diva Dwelling must be unique to you and your community.

REAL LIFE REAL ESTATE LESSONS

Sherry Chris
CEO, Better Homes and Gardens Real Estate
@sherrychris

I was drawn to the real estate industry 30 years ago as a first-time homebuyer. As I went through each step of the home buying process, I thought to myself, "I can do what my agent is doing, but I can do it better." So, I set out to make a career change and started my journey into the real estate world.

At that point in my life, I did not envision how greatly this career would challenge me and help me grow and cultivate my individual goals and values by inspiring curiosity and passion in my life. Today, I can't imagine working in any other industry, and am so energized to be at the helm of such a dynamic, forward-looking brand – Better Homes and Gardens® Real Estate.

I have always prided myself on being committed to my work and, in return, my work has given me the strength and satisfaction to keep me motivated every day.

The real estate community offers opportunities to be an entrepreneur at every level. The flexibility in the industry to challenge oneself and create one's own goals can be exhilarating and rewarding. As an agent, you become an independent contractor, holding yourself responsible for the work you are doing. The success you achieve is reached exclusively by your own efforts and that should not be forgotten as new roles are taken, however, the value of collaboration and teamwork should never be underestimated at any point in one's career – there are always opportunities to learn.

Along the way, the next generation of real estate professionals will find, as I have, that it is absolutely necessary to ground oneself in strong values in the pursuit of happiness and success. Throughout the course of my career, I have learned many lessons that have not only crafted who I am as a person, but also as a business leader and member of the real estate community. The key is to identify a passion and challenge yourself to think differently to help strengthen your industry and bring it into the future.

After three decades, I offer you the following guidance as you work to achieve greatness.

Be humble

On the way to the top, do not lose sight of the virtue of respect. Work selflessly and aim to give more than you expect to receive.

When I began my early career in Canada, I made a promise to myself that no matter what happened, I would continue to grace the community with a sense of humility and unassuming pride. Grandstanding your accomplishments will only make them less valuable to others. Instead, share and collaborate openly and unselfishly. Be open to learn from others, even your competitors, and never stop. I am still learning new things everyday and enjoy my role as both teacher and student.

There will always be competition. The key is to acknowledge that your competitors are also your peers, and they will be just as passionate as you are about the industry. Always respect your competitors. You are never going to be the only kid in the playground. So, get out there and learn how to play nicely with the others. I am fortunate to be part of a community filled with forward-thinking professionals who not only care about what they do, but also truly care about the people they are helping and working with. Building interpersonal relationships and remaining open will ultimately bring value and joy to your success. Remain humble and you will enjoy building meaningful relationships.

Be committed

Creating a successful career in any business is not always easy. Throughout my career, the real estate industry has seen its fair share of ups and downs. You should approach the most challenging situations with tenacity and examine new ways to overcome and succeed. Success may not be immediate, but this approach will be beneficial in the long run.

Every professional faces rough times, and it's essential to have the dedication to never give up on your dream. There are many things in life you can't control. In my case, we launched the national brand of Better Homes and Gardens Real Estate in 2008, just as the subprime mortgage crisis swept through the real estate industry. I didn't let the economic situation stop our growth. We worked harder and only concerned ourselves with what we could control, and for our first five years we have been one of the fastest growing national real estate brands in the country.

Surround yourself with greatness

Build an A-team and empower them to do great things. Your team should grow and evolve as your company grows, but they are your support system and their strength lies in your encouragement and direction. Be exceedingly picky in choosing whom you want to represent you and your brand.

When it comes to building a strong, stable environment, you must trust your instincts and learn to hire slowly and fire quickly. It's not easy, but don't be afraid to let someone go if it is for the betterment of the team. As long as you treat everyone with respect, as a leader, you have the power to choose who will stand by your side.

Become a teacher and share your knowledge with your team. At the same time, look for your own coaches that can provide you with a high level of accountability. My mentors have guided me throughout my career and taught me invaluable lessons. I would not be in my position without the support of my team and guidance of my mentors.

Be fearless

Be fearless in the pursuit of new ideas and remain unafraid to take calculated risks. Create a vision that is unique to your industry, company and clients, then make it happen. Do not be afraid of failing. Your greatest success stories will often parallel your greatest risks.

Throughout my career I have taken many risks, which in retrospect were absolutely necessary to my growth and that of the company. Regardless of whether they succeeded or failed, there was undeniable value in the endeavor.

Establish values

One of the first things I did when we built the Better Homes and Gardens Real Estate brand was to create a set of core business values, which we call PAIGE: Passion, Authenticity, Innovation, Growth, and Excellence.

These values stay with me in every aspect of my life, and they are qualities that are consistent across my team and our franchise network. Building a brand is very similar to building a home. You need to have the foundation set before constructing the walls.

In life, as in business, you are going to be presented with different challenges and obstacles that will determine and shape your reputation. Be true to yourself and true to others, and you will find success in real estate or in any field you choose. You will find that your reputation precedes itself as you continue to give back to others and openly foster a community of collaboration.

Do not put on a façade, but rather strive to be the same person inside and out, doing what you say you will do. I've learned, when you do things differently, you have an obligation to share for the betterment of all.

In closing, love what you do. If something isn't making you happy in work or in life, then find a way to fix it. There is always a way. It may not be easy and it may not be immediately apparent, but it will be worth it.

SUCCESS AND THE PURSUIT OF MAKING MONEY

Marc Davison
Partner, 1000watt
@1000wattmarc

I ripped open the nondescript package jutting out of my mailbox, revealing Gary Keller's book *Shift*, neatly tucked inside. A note was attached not dissimilar to past notes pasted to the books he's sent me over the years.

I've always admired Gary. He's a self-made guy. No one handed him anything.

I placed Gary's book on the chair in the den. I'd find the right spot for it in the bookcase later on. It would reside unopened among the other business books I've been sent over the years and never read. I've skimmed a few. Blue Ocean Strategy. Good to Great. Delivering Happiness. Perhaps a few more, but I don't read them.

I guess I'm wired differently than most. I don't measure success with the typical yardstick. Riches. Fame. Fortune. The results of success that often come at a cost that carry too much weight on the P&L of life.

I would never devalue the motivational or inspirational factor these books offer. But often, missing from their narratives, are the lesser known truths about success.

I left the book unattended.

Days later, Gary popped up inside my inbox. Did I get the book? What do I think? I glided into the den to fetch it, scan it and respond to Gary with a perspicacious response. The book was gone. My wife probably shelved it, I thought. Given the volume of books we possess covering two full walls, I decided to move on and let Gary know I'll dig into it soon. A commitment I planned to keep.

Later that night, at dinner, my eldest son asked me how I knew Gary Keller. "So you saw the book he sent?" I asked. He did and subsequently read the entire thing cover to cover in two days. After he promptly decided he was going to become a real estate agent.

Ryan graduated high school a year later. He moved to Portland in the fall to attend real estate school. He received his license in Oregon as a broker then immediately moved back home to

California where he passed that state's real estate exam.His next step, move to Orange County. Join a brokerage. Sell expensive homes. And get rich.

Just like Gary. Books motivate. *Shift* surely lit his fire. Filling his head with big dreams. When I asked him why he wanted to sell homes, he said, "So I can make bank."

Gary once told me that there's nothing wrong with making a lot of money so long as you do good things with it. Sadly, that advice was absent from the book. But even sadder was the absence of advice regarding the good things a person must do along the road to riches. Things that preserve a person's integrity in the pursuit of making money. The things that ensure a lifetime of success.

What I shared with my son that day was something you don't often read in best-selling business books or even think to seek out when creating your business plan This is what I offered:

True success is defined by how victorious you are in the battle over your inherent beliefs, morals, and values. The less of these you compromise for money, the more successful you'll be.

Success is ending every day knowing that you treated someone better than you expect to be treated yourself.

Success is recognizing mistakes, owning up to them, and taking every step to ensure they never happen again. Success comes at the conclusion of a task done flawlessly.

Success occurs when you confront a challenge rather than cower from it. You'll understand the value of this as you conquer difficulties and emerge better, stronger and smarter as a result. You witness success when people find more value in you as result.

Success is managing your disappointment with class.

Success is never selling a service you aren't 100% specialized at and referring a client to someone who is. True success is doing this and not taking a dime for it. In fact, that's something people describe as honorable.

Success is making commitments to people and sticking to them, come hell or high water.

Success is never compromising your ideals. Ever. Success occurs when you relentlessly stick to this and become known for it. True success comes from reaching a point where you no longer have to sell yourself because so many others vouch for you. Willingly. And intensely.

Success comes from sharing credit with your team rather than taking all the glory.

Success is all about recognizing your weaknesses and partnering with entities that possess strength in those areas. True success is deciding that the cost to do this is a prudent investment into your clients' well being. And your reputation.

Adhere to these things, and you will truly know success.

So, I made my son a deal. Go to SoCal. Do not sell a single house for one year. We'd support him along the way. Pay his rent. His gas. Insurance. Food. In return, he should tag along with pros. Do their open houses. Door knock. Watch how contracts are done. Over and over. He should continue his education. Creative writing. Marketing. Business law. Communications. Economics - the things required to be a responsible agent.

Get good. Then get great. Because real estate isn't a game. You represent real estate affairs. Shelter. The most important possession a person will buy in their lifetime. Don't just say those words. Feel them. Live them. Honor them.

Shortcuts, inferior tools, cutting corners not investing in yourself and your clients may be a standard badge of honor in real estate. Don't get sucked into that belief system. No one wins in the end.

This holds true for every act, action, process or decision you decide to take on in your career.

These things aren't taught in real estate school. They aren't shared in your weekly broker meetings. Or tweeted through social circles.

But they should be. Agents would be better served by it. As would the industry. And most importantly, those whom the industry serves. The customer.

CAREER ADVICE FOR MY DAUGHTER

Pete Flint
CEO, Trulia
@peteflint

My mother was a high school teacher and my father was an academic. Teaching and mentorship were lifelong passions for both and some of my favorite memories are those times when my parents would share things they had learned throughout their lives and careers.

Over the years, I've come to understand and appreciate just how valuable and impactful those lessons were, and as a new father myself, I plan to share much of the same wisdom with my own daughter. I hope to teach her how to change a tire and appreciate a good book, and foresee giving her sage advice on raising a family. I also hope to impart some professional wisdoms.

Here are some lessons I might share for the latter.

Dream big, but start small

When you embark on your career, you'll have high expectations and big dreams. This is a good thing. You'll frequently be surprised what you can achieve combining ambition and youth. A little naivete is most often an ally.

You're sure to face unforeseen challenges. At times, it may feel like there are limitless things that need your attention. However, don't let taxing experiences diminish your ambition or stifle your dreams. Every success, no matter how small, counts toward a larger goal.

Mind you, you won't be able to accomplish all your goals in one fell swoop. It's going to take time. Use each and every day to make consistent progress toward your goals.

Listen first

It's amazing how much you can learn about a person if you simply give him a chance to speak. Whether you're in real estate, medicine, or even engineering, lending someone your rapt attention will always serve you well. Indeed, true leadership is not about speaking first or speaking the loudest. An effective leader gathers information to make informed decisions.

For example, when building Trulia, my team and I made a special effort to reach out to our industry and understand its principal challenges. We had an idea of what we wanted to build, but listening first helped us immeasurably. To this day, we solicit feedback to help fashion our strategy.

Find a mentor

Mentors are the unsung heroes of the business world, fundamental to any successful career. In my experience, behind every good business deal is counsel from a mentor. Many people in your life can (and will) offer advice. However, truly great advice comes from an advisor who knows your strengths and weaknesses.

Always do your best

Always performing as well as you can may sound like pat and obvious advice, but it may be the most important guidance I can proffer. Nobody is perfect. You will make mistakes. I know that I have. But a mistake made while putting forth a best effort motivates rather than deters. Moreover, if you always do your best, you are sure to be noticed and offered unique opportunities. Striving, you'll also find more fulfillment in everything you do.

Dream big, listen first, learn from your peers, and do your best. If you do these things, I will be more proud of you than you can imagine.

TIME
AIN'T ON
YOUR SIDE

Nobu Hata
NAR Director of Digital Engagement
@nobuhata

It's been a little more than a year since I hung up my sales license to manage an association. As I write this, I find myself missing the grind. The 20-hour work days. The Multiple Listing Service research. The hours in the car previewing and showing homes. And the open houses. And while I no longer help buyers realize their home ownership dreams, I now counsel my former peers to help clients do just that, sharing my sales and leadership experience.

But it's hard. It's hard to properly convey to my coworkers how difficult it is to be an agent in the digital age; or what it feels like to have a buyer cry her eyes out because she lost a home in multiple offers for the third time; or how strange it is to justify your value to a seller who thinks sales data found with a smartphone application is gospel. More difficult still is answering the perennial question,

"How do I succeed in real estate?" As a former salesperson, nerd, leader, and now association staffer, folks expect me to share the wisdom of the ages. But there is no silver bullet, no magic technique. Likewise, there's no coup by social media, nor a toppling of the industry by the Internet. Agents need not be paperless.

In fact, if there is a systemic problem, it's time. Too much time is spent on thinking and not enough on acting. Not enough time is spent with clients, while too much is spent on the Next Big Shiny Thing. Really, that's the crux of issue: too much time is spent on things instead of people. Personal interaction — face-to-face and belly-to-belly — is the one thing that no website or online campaign can synthesize or usurp, and it's time well spent. And (at least for now), you can't be cloned. It's the little things that you do every day that can set you apart from your competitors and make a difference in your marketing. Some suggestions.

Use that phone in your pocket to capture your volunteering. Share that hidden gem of a neighborhood playground. Show off your favorite dog park. Share your expertise as well. Use your blog to educate, demystify, and explain. It's time we told our current and future clients what's important in a real estate transaction.

No one deals with more unique situations than a realtor. No one deals with more adversity or rolls with the punches better than a realtor. And there is no one that works harder for his or her client than a realtor.

PERSEVERANCE ABOVE ALL ELSE

Dottie Herman

President and CEO, Douglas Elliman Real Estate

@dottieherman

People say that you have to do what you love to be successful at it. That's especially true in real estate because it's a 24-hour, seven-day-a week passion, not a nine-to-five job. In today's world, everything is about real estate. Owning a home is the heart of the American Dream, and real estate is the financial engine that drives our economy.

The challenge in real estate, like it is in life, is not about being good, it's about going from good to great. That takes not only hard work but personal courage. The greatest piece of wisdom I can impart about being successful is that you can't be afraid to fail, no matter how big your dreams are, or how insurmountable the obstacles may seem. I would never have been able to put together one of the largest real estate companies in the world if I had been held back by fear of failing. It's not that I haven't suffered disappointments, but set-backs aren't failure. Success is failure inside out.

Most importantly, you need a clear and consistent vision of your goals. I never blindly moved from one thing to the next, yet I always left myself open as opportunities presented themselves to get me to where I wanted to go. I was never in a hurry. It's not realistic to expect instant gratification in a business career.

Like Aesop's tortoise, I knew that steady progress was more important than speed in crossing the finish line. If you asked me what my goal was from the start, I would say it was to build an integrated real estate company where a customer could get expert advice and guidance in every aspect of real estate, from financing, buying, selling, to commercial real estate, and property management.

Life is a series of defining moments, not all of them easy. These moments can be daunting, if you let them, or you can use them to help you grow and strengthen your resolve.

The moment that most shaped my life happened when I was only ten years old. My mother, father, and my younger sister and brother and I were on our way back from a Vermont skiing trip to our Long Island home when the car skidded off the road and my mother and I were thrown from the car. When I woke up in the hospital I was told by a priest that my father was seriously injured and my mother had died. It was devastating. When a 10-year old girl loses her mother, she changes. I occasionally wonder what my life would have been like if she hadn't died. Having no one to nurture me, I had to nurture myself and my father and my siblings, who turned to me for love and guidance. I grew up quickly.

I understood from an early age that life wasn't forever and you've got to make the best of your time. I resolved that I would make something of myself. I sent myself through college, I got my real estate license, and I went to work for Merrill Lynch, when they had a real estate division. As part of my job, I traveled throughout the country on behalf of the company, learning about the national real estate market, giving me invaluable insight into the business that has served me well to this day.

Another defining moment presented itself to me in 1989. Merrill Lynch had sold their real estate division to Prudential, and two years later, Prudential decided it was going to sell off regional holdings, including the Long Island offices. I decided I wanted to buy the entire Long Island division. People said I was crazy.

First of all, I had no money to buy it. If I wanted to buy a single office it would have been one thing, but I wanted to buy all of Long Island. I'll admit it was pretty brazen, but if you want something, you have to ask for it, so I convinced Prudential to loan me the money to buy the Long Island franchise for $9 million. In effect, they had enough faith in me (and my track record) to finance my purchase of their own company.

In the early 1990s I bought a house in the Hamptons, a place I loved. It was always my dream to have a weekend place on the East End of Long Island. It's one of the most exquisite locations in the country, only two hours from Wall Street, and it will never go out of style. It's also one of the most active real estate markets. In the real estate business, the Hamptons is like Monopoly's Park Place and Boardwalk combined. Once I owned a home there, how could I not want to open a real estate office?

Again, people warned me I would fail trying to expand into the Hamptons because the real estate business was dominated by a group of local real estate companies who were fiercely protective of their turf. But I never focus on my competitors; I focus on my goals and follow my customers. In 2003, I opened the first Hamptons office of my company from scratch, recruiting a local salesforce, and creating a full-service company with offices in every village and hamlet. Within 10 years of hard work and determination, the company became the leader in real estate sales on the entire East End of Long Island.

But I wasn't done. The greatest prize of all was still across the East River. I always knew that one day I would open offices in

New York. Long before I opened in the Hamptons, the company's website said "from Montauk to Manhattan." The challenge was that Long Island real estate companies were always separate from Manhattan. The East River was supposed to be impassable for a Long Island-based real estate company. Much like the Hamptons, the city had its own entrenched real estate companies, but I contended that if Robert Moses could build bridges and roadways between Long Island and Manhattan, I could bridge the gap with one real estate company.

In 2003, in a move that stunned the New York real estate community and made headlines, I purchased one of the oldest and most esteemed companies in the business, Douglas Elliman, for nearly $72 million, with my business partner, Howard Lorber. Douglas Elliman is now the fourth largest real estate company in the United States, with over 6,000 agents and employees, 70 offices, $12 billion dollars a year in sales, and offices in Miami and Palm Beach.

Success and the realization of my dreams is thrilling, but the real satisfaction isn't about how quickly I became successful or how successful I became, it's about how I got there. Perseverance. The bottom line is, are you better today than you were yesterday?

My success is about a series of steps forward, some small, some giant leaps. Real estate is one of the most exciting businesses in the world, tremendously rewarding both emotionally and financially, but it's also competitive and tough. If you love what you're doing, the rest is superfluous.

THE CHINA SYNDROME

Tina Mak

Broker, Coldwell Banker Westburn Realty

@tinamak

The fall of the Berlin Wall ushered in a period of profound global political transformation and economic liberalization. Previously closed economies joined the community of trading nations. This has created a new burgeoning middle class in developing countries. Nowhere has the positive and far reaching consequences of this new reality been more apparent than in China.

Powered by the Internet, the information society has transformed the global economy in ways we could not have previously imagined. Everything is now mobile: People travel freely between countries; data is open and shared at warp speed; trillions in various currencies are transferred instantaneously at the touch of a button. Borders and nationalities are less relevant than they ever have been. Technology has made our world a much smaller and tighter community. Globalization is not just a buzzword; it's an ever-present reality.

The astounding potential of this economic reality still has not fully sunk in for most observers and policy makers. China is now the second largest economy on earth. That growth will continue at a robust pace.

As a region, Asia is a more substantial than at any other time in the history of civilization. Yet to many in the West, it remains a mystery. Some view China, for instance, with fear. Others view it as an immense opportunity to create wealth, prosperity, and bring people closer together.

The rise of a massive and growing middle class in China is an entirely new phenomena. We've seen the early impact. Armed with savings and disposable income, an increasing number of Chinese have entered the North American real estate market. Some families are looking for a safe-haven for their life savings, others seek a place to retire. As prosperity spreads and China's economy grows, another 600 million people are striving to reach middle class status.

While this undoubtedly creates challenges for Chinese policy makers, it represents a tremendous opportunity for those of us in the real estate industry in North America's West Coast. British Columbia, Washington, Oregon, and California are highly favored destinations for Chinese investors. The communities are livable, safe, accommodating, and welcoming. The weather is temperate— winters are neither too cold nor too hot. Relative to world markets, these locations offer tremendous value. And of course, the geography is among the most spectacular on the planet.

Canada has been a very attractive destination for overseas real estate buyers. The stability of the political and investment climate, relatively low prices, and the sheer beauty of the country has generated robust activity compared to other key markets.

Of those making Canada a preferred destination, investors from China and India have flocked to British Columbia and the greater Vancouver region. Over twenty-five per cent of residents in Greater Vancouver, Canada's third largest metropolitan region after Toronto and Montreal, speak Chinese as a first language.

So far, the Chinese have not been a dominant player in all sectors of real estate; their investments have typically been focused within China itself. However, Chinese citizens have been investing in London, Singapore, Sydney, and New York. And in recent years, they have intensified their activity in North America's Pacific region. There are signs that Chinese buyers are setting sights eastward, too, in search of long-term value and returns on investment.

Mainland Chinese, now cash rich, are actively searching for new places to deploy their capital. In June 2013, Sun Hung Kai Properties, Hong Kong's largest developer, sold almost 90 per cent of units on offer in Hong Kong for its River Green project in

Vancouver within a month when it debuted last month. Centaline Property said that about half of those sales went to Chinese buyers. The *South China Morning Post* reported that Hong Kong's overseas property transactions jumping nearly 50 per cent in May 2013 from a year earlier, of which Mainland Chinese made up a fifth of sales.

All of this is driving a paradigm shift in the way real estate agents deal with the newly affluent and middle-class client from China.

Money does have direction, though. It flows, as always, where the best returns can be found. Money is dispassionate and today has no borders. Money is objective, unemotional, and wholly lacking in prejudice. Its one and only criteria is the search for the best return at the lowest possible risk.

I am often asked how to do business with Chinese clients. Being intimately familiar with the language, culture, and mindset of your client is an indispensible attribute. If you don't understand your client or have the capacity to communicate with them, you are at a serious competitive disadvantage. But beyond that obvious truism, in the final analysis, Chinese buyers are really no different than anyone else: The Chinese client wants to trust the person they are doing business with.

Being successful in the real estate business is no different than what it takes to be a successful contributor in any other business.

A few very basic principles transcend this industry. In a nutshell they can be summarized as:

1. Know your customer better than anyone
2. Know your market better than anyone
3. Know your product better than anyone
4. Know the economics of getting to "yes"
5. Know the broad macro factors which affect those four factors
6. Always be straight and honest in your dealings with people

While borders matter less today, relationships have never been more important. Building relationships based on trust must become a fixation, requiring thinking and acting with a decidedly long term, not short term, outlook. In my experience, I have found that an emphasis on the short term might very well land you a sale, but chances are won't nurture a sustainable business.

This perspective also means that you must be honest, sometimes brutally and relentlessly so, with advice and opinions. I treat my clients the way I want to be treated: as an intelligent person that takes my hard earned money very seriously. Like the clients I typically work with, I expect facts and analysis with a bare minimum of sugarcoating.

Asians, which in my definition broadly includes Middle Eastern, South East Asian, and Chinese, are all tough and direct negotiators. We're also social animals. We typically prefer to make a deal in a social environment. The common denominator among us is that we like to feel that we have "won" in any negotiation. "Face" is critically important.

Those seeking a principal residence are the easiest to work with. Those making a pure real estate investment, focused on the bottom line, are skilled negotiators. The latter are typically very savvy and experienced investors, which means they are tough and demanding customers.

There are a variety of ways to reach out to buyers from China and the rest of Asia. They range from immigration consultants & lawyers, agents in China for international students, travel agencies, and franchise owners in Asia. Of course, one of the most reliable is the good, old-fashioned referral.

There are generally two types of clients in the market for a principal residence. Those who invest to obtain a US Green Card (or Landed Immigrant status in Canada), usually look for comfort, and a luxury home to display their affluence and status. These clients are typically willing to spend a bit more. They also want space, meaning a lot of land, which the typical Asian finds highly desirable, largely because it is so rare in the native country. Despite their toughness as negotiators, Chinese are often willing to overpay for land because of their belief that it is safe, secure, and always rises in value.

Ironically, don't ask them to pay for an architect and designer to build a high quality home! If they do agree to hire a designer, make sure the person can communicate with them in their language. Chinese tastes are very distinct and are not best served by Western designers. In my experience, furnished properties sometimes solve the headache.

The second type of client is those who immigrate as skilled workers. These clients don't have deep pockets. preferring to buy something less expensive first and upgrade later.

But in both cases, these potential buyers are interested in newer properties and seldom look at anything over ten years old.

An increasing number of sophisticated Chinese are active investors and seek to protect and even extract a meaningful return on capital. While the range and depth of data points and analysis naturally increases with this kind of customer, the general approach is the same: they want the best possible deal and will fight hard to get it. We Chinese are very shrewd investors. To gain the trust of the Chinese buyer and investor, you must be as smart and tough as they are.

As I write this, Chinese investors are holding their collective breaths to see if the banking crisis predicted by Chinese economist Li Zuojun will come to pass. Li's past forecasting accuracy has earned him the nickname "China's most successful doomsayer."

Li also says that housing prices will collapse. Speculation has it that new Chinese president Xi Jinping will maintain tight controls to ensure that any drop in housing prices will not be too dramatic, possibly limited to about 10-20%. However, Li says that a United States-like collapse is not out of the question.

The potential economic and political implications of a Chinese failure can cause buyers a case of the jitters. But it can also mean buyers export capital to safe havens, such as the North American real estate market. Either way, I know two things for sure: China's economic might will be a powerful contributor to a new dynamic in the North American real estate landscape; and we have no choice but to get used to and try to take advantage of the seismic abnormalities of this new normal.

Emerging economies will continue to grow for the foreseeable future, fueled by a new, educated and sophisticated middle class. This newly prosperous constituency will aggressively seek out investments in North American real estate.

So while the global economy adjusts and expands to this new normal, there is uncertainty, but for the entrepreneurial realtor, a magnificent reward waits to be seized.

THE GOLDEN RULES OF REAL ESTATE

Michael McClure

CEO, VerifiedAgent.com

@professionalone

I have so many thoughts and ideas and impulses for someone about to embark on a life-long career in real estate. Here are the biggest things that come to mind:

Be honest

Whether we're talking about a career in real estate or a career in any other industry, your reputation is really all you have.

A great reputation is the single greatest attribute, characteristic, or asset any real estate professional can possess. Always go the extra mile, not only to be honest, but to avoid any hint or appearance of impropriety.

Be competent

Let me speak plainly here. If a person wanted to, and their ethics were less-than-perfect, they could have a reasonably okay career in real estate by doing a fairly mediocre job. It's way too easy to get a real estate license, and the sad reality is that most brokers will accept just about anyone who shows up at their door with a license and a pulse.

Sadly, with its low barrier to entry, poor enforcement of the National Association of Realtors® Code of Ethics and the strong allure of "big, easy money" (and further exacerbated by the unfortunate ignorance on the part of much of the public in terms of how to choose a great agent), the industry all but invites marginally competent people to come and join the party. Do not succumb to the easy opportunity to be mediocre. Always strive to provide exceptional service to each and every client, and to be a true professional. Never stop mastering your craft.

Be professional

Demonstrate professionalism in all things at all times. Lead by example and strive to elevate those around you with your complete commitment to excellence. Real estate is often chaotic, fragmented, disjointed, poorly communicated, misunderstood, misinterpreted, dramatic, high stress and last-minute.

It is very easy to lose one's composure and behave in a less than professional fashion. Always keep your composure. Always keep your cool. Always do your best to see the other side of every issue and situation.

Be a true fiduciary

In most states, agents function as fiduciaries. In such situations, our clients' interests supersede our interests. Real estate is full of opportunities where you can increase your chances of earning income by looking the other way or by not disclosing something or by not passing along a comment which might impact your client's behavior or affect their ultimate decision making in one way or another.

We must always put our clients' interests above our own. That is legally required in situations where we function as fiduciaries. Please take that obligation to heart and let it dictate your every decision.

Be golden

Practice the "Golden Rule" with respect to everyone at all times— your clients, other agents, other agents' clients and the general public. Always treat everyone the way you would want to be treated. Make your enemy your friend. Many people in the real estate industry for some reason think that representing their clients' interests requires them to behave in an adversarial fashion.

I happen to disagree with that. I believe that extreme diplomacy is the path to the greatest level of success in the highest percentage of situations. And when your peers come to see you as reasonable and objective, they will begin to go out of their way to do business with you. And when that starts to happen, it can take your business to an entirely new level.

Keep learning

Never be satisfied with mediocrity. Never stop improving, growing and learning. Know your weaknesses and work hard to overcome them. This is true not only for the obvious issues affecting professional competency, but also "outside" things like Social Media and video and blogging and things of that nature. It's been said that social media is the greatest cultural shift since the Industrial Revolution, and I happen to agree.

Our world is changing radically, and we have to stay current to understand and react to those changes. I believe that real competitive advantage awaits those who leverage these changes most effectively. The huge popularity of Facebook and Twitter, with 1 billion and 300 million users, respectively, speaks volumes about the significance of these changes.

Over-deliver

As a consumer who has worked with many service professionals, doctors, lawyers, CPAs and real estate agents, namely, I can tell you that people simply doing what they tell you they're going to do is important. Massively important. So many people today are guilty of over-promising and under-delivering that it's become almost "the norm" and culturally acceptable. That's a bad thing.

Always be super conservative when discussing timetables and deadlines. Take what you think the deadline is really going to be and add a day or two or three or maybe even a week. And then get things done ahead of those deadlines. I have found that this is one of the quickest and easiest ways to gain the long-term trust and confidence of clients.

Be relational

The very best agents that I know do little or no advertising or lead generation. And if you know anything about real estate, you know that that it is highly unusual, as many agents spend thousands if not tens of thousands of dollars every year on advertising and promotion of one kind or another, and "lead gen" is something that consumes the majority of many agents' work days.

So, how do these agents get away with not spending a lot of money promoting themselves or on lead generation? The answer is surprisingly obvious: they focus on creating real, tangible and legitimate relationships with each and every client and they provide amazing service to every buyer and every seller. They make every client a raving fan.

I was fortunate enough to enter the industry being mentored by a veteran agent of this kind. She's been in the business now over 35 years, and I haven't seen her spend a dime on promotion for the last 15 years. And she doesn't even understand what "lead gen" means. And she has more clients than she can handle. It's all because of her exceptional devotion to relationship creation and maintenance. As a real-life illustration of this, my mentor has one past client that has referred well over 50 clients to us, almost all of whom are in the $400K+ range (and several of whom are in the $1M+ range). That "referral tree" is now three or four levels deep, and has produced well over $500K in gross commission income - from ONE raving fan past client! And that was built by nothing more than providing great service and focusing on the relationship more than the sale.

Be positive

Even for the best agents, real estate is often a bit of a roller coaster ride. Clients do unexpected, crazy things. Deals that you thought were solid fall apart at the last minute. People often behave in illogical and frustrating ways. Through it all, strive to keep a positive attitude.

This is another thing that I learned from my mentor. I saw people treat her poorly yet she always turned the other cheek. More often than not, the people who treated her poorly found a way to repay her in the long run. People know when they mistreat you, and it often happens in the heat of the moment, when they are under pressure or when emotions are running high. When you take the high road and keep a positive attitude, it's amazing how often wrongs get righted.

Take the long view

I'm a big believer that the length of one's perspective is really important. What I mean by that is that if you're making decisions based upon the short-term view, you may very well make different decisions than if you take a longer view of whatever the situation might be. This goes hand-in-hand with my earlier point about focusing on the relationship and not the transaction, but I'll risk the redundancy just to make the point again.

When we focus on the longest term view of any situation, we tend to make better decisions and take more appropriate actions. The long view is the *only* view. Always base decisions on the long-term implications.

Be self-determinant

I could easily be wrong about this, but I can't think of any other industry that is more "self determinant" than real estate. It is really important as you enter the industry to understand that. Can you get help from others? Of course you can. You should make a real effort to find a great broker and a great company to help you get started in the right direction in your career. But in the long run, it's all about you, your efforts and your willingness to do what it takes to be successful in a highly competitive and super dynamic environment. The best agents are self-motivated and almost always tend to be successful because of their own efforts.

Be tenacious

I remember stumbling upon a survey a few years ago, intended to reveal the most important characteristic in terms of being able to predict success in the real estate industry. The survey showed that tenacity was the number one predictor of success in real estate. So, be tenacious. Never give up. Never stop trying. When you encounter problems, stumbling blocks, and challenges, dig your heels in and simply make up your mind to overcome them.

Follow the leaders

Social media has given us an amazing, unprecedented opportunity to connect with almost literally anyone, including the very brightest and most influential people in the real estate industry. I could give you a monster list of people I think you should follow, but that would take up this entire chapter. Follow the best and the brightest and just learn all you can from them.

Three people I must name specifically are Stefan Swanepoel (@Swanepoel), Marc Davison (@1000WattMarc) and Krisstina Wise (@KrisstinaWise). I've learned so much from these three. Just follow them and you'll see. Also, I suggest you follow Erik Qualman (@Equalman), who is not in real estate but who is one of the world's foremost authorities on Social Media.

Communicate

I saved this point for last, because, after "be honest," this is the most important point of all. Great agents are great communicators. There is so much room for miscommunication that you simply must err on the side of over-communication.

As a broker, I can tell you that the vast majority—I'd say as much as 90%—of all problems in transactions can be traced back to some variety of miscommunication. Never assume. Always ask. Always communicate.

This overview are just highlights of what paths can lead you to success, but anyone who incorporates all of these things into their real estate career is likely to be very successful.

THE REAL ESTATE STARTUP

Kelly Mitchell
Founder, Agent Caffeine
@kellymitchell

I've been in Hawaii most of my life. From my extensive tenure here, I have learned of the limited opportunity for a career. You can't drive to another state and sell people stuff. You can't even drive to another island. When you're here, you are here, especially if you're on a budget, a student, or building a career.

Most think people get into the real estate industry because they're looking for more freedom or they had a career change. For me, I had just faced the dot com implosion and survived... Barely.

I honestly thought, with my entrepreneurial and tech background real estate would be a breeze. Needing an income I had come to a crossroads. Real estate would be perfect. Right?! I'd do it part-time while I was figuring out "the next big thing". How difficult could it be to show houses? Doesn't everyone need one? Show a house, write an offer, collect a check. Easy!

I quickly discovered the folly of my reasoning. Next I learned I was back in the middle of yet another startup. Yep. Becoming an agent is just like starting a new company. WAIT. No one told me I actually had to work it just like any other start up...

I really didn't think of real estate as a startup. I didn't understand the long, tough road ahead. I thought for sure my friends and family would buy from me immediately. I also felt that people who met me who loved my engaging personality would overlook inexperience and hire me immediately. Little did I know, many of the people who I crossed paths with already knew anywhere from 10 to 12 other agents. You see, on Oahu alone, there are 6,000 agents. The most isolated land mass in the world has an island with 6,000 real estate agents.

In fact, there were so many agents here that when I would open my mouth and say I was in real estate, it was one of the quickest conversation killers in the circles that I ran in. Everyone had a license.

I buckled down and focused. Systems were important to me, so I thought finding a company that focused on systems and technology would be a huge advantage. If I have those two things, anything was possible.

I joined a local franchise of a national affiliate – they had the tech systems in place I needed and they were the leader in the vertical

A PATH TO PASSION, PURPOSE, AND PROFITS IN REAL ESTATE

here in tech. On reflection, that didn't mean much, but it was a motivator just the same. They had 30 years already in the industry and the data to come with it, a very powerful asset for prospecting.

So there I was at square one. I didn't start out with the right mind set, but choosing the right company was key. This was the foundation of how I built my success. Beyond that, who you are, how you think, your nature, and ability to be creative are other strong elements. The right company is part of success, but without your own drive and determination, you might end up like the majority of the other people in my training class... out of the business in less than two years.

Learning what works for you and not trying to be somebody you're not is critically important to success. What I learned was that certain things worked for me in this business (phone calls, face to face meetings, open houses, working web leads), others did not (answering phone calls off of ads that someone else wrote, cold calling, door knocking and being a 'salesperson'). I've never been very good at faking anything. Honest to a fault and an open book unless negotiating. Authenticity is key.

A powerful ingredient once I had success, was to make sure I understood how success was generated. Tracking my activities was key to understanding that. I used to get so frustrated at my coach. I'd go into her office and ask, "What's everyone else doing that's making them successful?" and she'd reply, "Doing the daily activities that lead to a sale, and knowing the daily activities that work for you."

I was always hoping for the silver bullet, that one thing that was the magic. The truth is that the one thing is YOU. The magic is you knowing what to do.

I focused on my strengths and what I enjoyed. That approach is what makes winners persevere. The truth is that the gap between being very successful and modestly successful is not that big. The major difference is your level of focus, support, and resilience. I Reflect on the things that yield a successful closing and replicate it again and again.

Out of the things I was best at, what I disliked the most was picking up the phone those first 2-3 times of a day. Once I got past the third call, it was always a breeze. When I made it a competition with myself, if became fun, and something I had to win. So if it's a game you need to create to make it fun, do it. You know yourself best. Create an environment of opportunity and fun. It makes all the difference!

I want to be candid and share that I made mistakes. The first and biggest mistake I made was I did not own a niche. I became successful in spite of that, but oh how much more successful I would have been if I owned a niche in the market's mind, in the prospect's mind, and in my client's mind. Another glorious mistake: I once took on a horrible client who I didn't get along with and we both lacked respect for each other.

I made one silly mistake, which was forgetting to invite his mortgage person to the signing (the mortgage paperwork was all done), and he screamed at me in our corporate office at the top of his lungs for about 30 minutes. That was a turning point. This isn't about the money. Do your deals with the right people. For the right reasons. Do not take deals that compromise your integrity or values or work with people lacking in that area. No money in the world is worth it. That blood sucker temporarily cost self-confidence, sanity, peace of mind, and he humiliated me. Wait! Shame on me. I let him. No commission check in the world is worth working with people who don't respect you.

I've also wasted tens of thousands of dollars on promises of secret ingredients for the most exclusive "deal" for advertising, or getting leads, but don't fall for it – you won't be the coolest Realtor in the coupon book.

The magic is you, it's not an ad, it's not your pretty picture on a shopping cart, a bus, a billboard. It's not how big your picture is on Trulia. The basics are always the best way to build and sustain a business. Take advantage of systems. Don't do paperwork. Good lord, don't do paperwork. You are the rainmaker. Focus on rainmaker activities. Talk to other agents that are willing to share with you what's working for them. Build a support system outside of your region with other agents. Build your tribe so you can share ideas, successes, and failures, and help each other when the going gets tough. Do not fear the competition. They can be an asset when the right relationships are cultivated.

Today, I'm at a place where I've found balance and have a strong desire to help others not repeat the mistakes I have made over the years. I want to accelerate their growth, help them be happy, and lead them to find passion and joy in what they do.

I started with Agent Caffeine, which helps agents, business people, and entrepreneurs get a leg up on what's happening in business, strategy, communications, marketing, and digital. I've done 200+ interviews to date and continue to produce a minimum of two fresh episodes per week with thought-leaders in and out of real estate. I do this because I believe we need that combination to innovate and break free of old attitudes and ways.

In early 2013, I brought to life another vision for startups and entrepreneurs called BreveTV, a videocast. The series helps people learn so they don't have to struggle when they enter business or traverse industries. That's a key driver of mine. Hearing directly from people who have taken action in their business because of something you put your love, heart and soul into... that's magic for me. True success.

In my real estate career, I'm now very selective at how I pursue deals and clients, and it is the fuel that helps me fund my start-ups, my shows, my lifestyle—the things that drive me. My real estate business is driven 100% from referrals and I became an overnight success in eight years. Now I work with people like me. I want the process to be easier.

I may always keep my fingers in real estate. It gives me a richer perspective of what our pain points are and the pleasures. You can't understand it unless you've lived it (I don't care what "they" say).

The entrepreneurial aspects of Red Koi (my media company), BreveTV, and Agent Caffeine (my podcast properties) are what keep me going and excited about tomorrow. So it's time to ask yourself...

1. Why am I in this business?
2. What is my niche?
3. What makes me happy?
4. Who do I want to work with?
5. How can I be more efficient?
6. Where is my passion?
7. What support do I need to focus on being the rainmaker?
8. How can I start my day with the right attitude, a strong investment in my well-being, and visualizations I need to get to the next level?

Go forth and change your business to match your values and ideals. Pick your niche so you can work smarter. Use mobile technology to make the quality of your life and your client's life better. Paperless above all is powerful. What appears to be simple takes an incredible amount of hard work and perseverance to make it so.

REAL TALK

Tara-Nicholle Nelson
Founder, REThink Real Estate
@taranicholle

Over the past decade of my life, I've sold real estate and been a real estate attorney. I've listened to hundreds of buyers' dreams and life visions in the car, at their dining room tables and at the litigation table. I've also spoken and written about real estate on a much larger stage - the stage of national media. I have listened to millions of buyers' and sellers' issues, fears, triumphs, dramas, and dreams online.

I know a little something about this business, and I'd like to share with you some takeaways I think would have been useful to me when I was beginning my own real estate career.

Buckle up.

When it comes to marketing, there are lots of ways to be successful in this business. I know people who make seven figures working by referral only, while others have nailed the fine arts of online marketing, knocking on doors, farming with postcards, and even, as crazy as it sounds, putting their faces on bus benches. Even crazier, cold calling.

That said, what's crazier than these old school marketing methods is not having a well-built web presence and tending to your online reputation, even if you choose to focus your marketing efforts offline.

Here's the key: don't be addicted to immediacy. The agents who have thriving businesses and brands that generate qualified clients in all market climates are the ones who are consistent. Learn to manage your emotional reactions to not getting immediate results. Put a strategic marketing plan and goals in place every year, and then work the plan. Tweak the plan. But don't abandon the plan before it has a chance to pay off.

Managing your emotions and your mindset is part and parcel of running a thriving, sustainable real estate business. Prayer and meditation are sanity-saving practices in a business that can mess with your mind, if you're not careful. Create a habit of paying yourself first by devoting your first waking hour or so to quiet time and self-care, attending to both your physical fitness and emotional wellness.

Managing your personal finances is equally important. Living well within your means, saving and investing, paying your taxes on time and avoiding debt empowers you to avoid panic, fear and paralysis while you're building your brand, ramping up your marketing and when the market slows down.

Because the market will slow down. Listen - more than most, I'm a big believer in the power of positive self-talk, the practice of declaring what you want to be as though it already is the Biblical wisdom that the power of life and death are in the tongue. I believe in refusing to participate in recessions. But the agents who last are those who are brutally honest about the reality that the real estate market, like all economic markets, is cyclical.

Without losing hope or conceding to fear and doubt, they acknowledge these seasons. They plan for the down markets, position for them and, thus, last through them. Be one of these agents.

And speaking of power, remember this: the transactions that you work on are the single-most powerful lifestyle transformation experience most of your clients will ever experience. Learn to think about what you do, this business of real estate, from the same perspective and to talk about it with the same vocabulary that your clients do. They are not looking to you only for the granular expertise on the nuts and bolts of how to find a home or do a deal.

They crave to level-up their lives. Their children's lives. Their financial futures. Their ability to care for their aging parents, build a thriving marriage - they need an ecosystem, a habitat for all of these things. That's what they want from you. If you can get them to entrust you with their holistic vision of life in the home you sell them (or sell for them), and if you show yourself worthy of that trust, coaching them through the real estate experience as a lifestyle transformation initiative, they will crave to consult with you for the rest of their lives. As will their family and friends.

If you fail at something, metabolize it quickly, just like your body metabolizes food. Keep only what's helpful, like the lessons and takeaways, and throw away the rest - the upset and angst.

And above all else, never be cheap when it comes to your vision. Vision is free, so don't be stingy! Without it, you'll flounder and even perish, in this business. Envision big. Know that everything is possible in this business and in your life. You are limitless. Onward and upward.

BECOMING A
TOP PRODUCER

Spencer Rascoff
CEO, Zillow
@spencerrascoff

The following is a letter addressed to my child and, in effect, to the next generation of youngsters we hope to guide into the real estate industry.

Dear Alan,

You've decided to become a real estate agent. Congratulations! You've chosen a great career, one in which you can leverage your entrepreneurial spirit, superior work ethic and warm personality to write your own ticket. This is an industry where the only limitation to your success is what you put into it. So the good news is the sky's the limit; the bad news is that being responsible for your own success is pressure-packed. But I know you're up to the challenge.

Without a doubt, being a real estate agent is challenging and it's not as clear-cut as just helping someone buy or sell a house.

You're forced to become an expert in a wide variety of fields, from contract law to website search engine optimization and negotiation to personal finance. Sometimes, it gets messy and you find yourself peripherally involved in marriage counseling and family planning.

And your range of knowledge and ability doesn't stop there. You have to become equally accomplished at setting up your own computer and getting your own health insurance as you are at helping a first-time home buyer navigate the incredibly harrowing transaction of buying a home. It's all details all the time and it's all on you.

I have never been a real estate agent, but I grew up in a real estate household where my mom (your grandmother) was an agent with Douglas Elliman in New York. Throughout my childhood, we went to open houses for fun and now I return the favor by dragging you and your siblings to open houses (perhaps the word "dragging" is a bit strong; you kids love the adventure as much as I did when I was your age and I still deeply enjoy attending open houses and learning about real estate). It's my weekend recreation, which helps my professional insight.

Nowadays, I sit on an interesting perch from which to dole out unsolicited advice. As CEO of the largest real estate website and suite of mobile apps, I am keenly aware of what separates successful agents from the rest. I see it all day long.

A PATH TO PASSION, PURPOSE AND PROFITS IN REAL ESTATE

So here goes.

Write a business plan

If you don't know how to write one, search for information online. By having a plan, you set a course for yourself and establish goals for where you want to be in one year, five years, etc. It helps establish a marketing plan and bring the industry into focus— who is your competition, who are your allies, etc.

Get a coach

Being a real estate agent is a lonely job and you'll need someone to push you to be better. Good real estate agent coaching services are expensive, but I've seen what a positive impact they can have on an agent. If you find a good one, it will pay for itself many times over.

Develop an Internet presence

This can be wide and all-encompassing, but with a little effort and patience, being online will pay big dividends -- especially in the form of online lead generation. Start with having your own personal website or blog and you can add social media into the mix later. But being online is vitally important. It's the way the world searches for information about anything and everything, including real estate.

Embrace transparency

Thanks to the Web, the world has opened up. Previously hard-to-access information is now available on the Web and that includes real estate info. A case in point is Zillow's Zestimate® home value. When the Zestimate rolled out in 2006, professionals in the real estate industry were not ready for it, but consumers were. People wanted transparency and information. Rather than reject the Zestimate, successful real estate pros saw the benefit – it was a way to open the conversation and be the expert.

Just like people use WebMD as a guide for health issues, they still want to see a doctor. With the Zestimate, it's a good starting point, but at some point most people will want to engage a professional. Be that person.

Accept feedback

Whether it's from a colleague or, especially clients you might have, be open to feedback about your performance. This can come in the form of online reviews and ratings. For example, Yelp can be a curse or a blessing for restaurants. But good restaurants will embrace reviews and ratings because if you have a great product, there is nothing to fear and everything to gain. Same for you. If you are confident in your abilities, you should seek reviews and ratings from clients. Let them tell your success story. Zillow was the first to offer ratings and reviews of agents and it's been a positive feature for consumers looking for agents, as well as agents themselves.

There are many other tips I can offer, but these are the primary tactics used by top-producing agents to dominate their market area. Just remember that since all real estate is local, you will need to explore what works well in your market and what doesn't. Don't be afraid to innovate and to test different kinds of marketing ideas. After all, this is your company and your business. It's up to you to make it happen and I know you will.

ADAPTATION

Marc Siden

CEO, Onboard Informatics

@markatonboard

They say the road to true peace is acceptance. Perhaps it's true that the path to managing through adversity in business follows the same principle. As the co-founder and CEO of a New York City self-funded start-up in its eleventh year in business, I sit in my office reflecting on where the curves in the road took us. It's easy in a way to see where adaptability has taken us. Much has changed in eleven years' time when I sat in this seat—which was a folding chair at the time—as my partner Jon Bednarsh and I built the business from the ground up, literally, in an East Village basement apartment.

Now overlooking the the Lower Manhattan skyline and harbor from my office, we are forever changed by what the market and our hundreds of clients have taught us about being adaptable over the years. My hope is that this chapter channels the lessons and battle scars learned along the way into manageable disciplines that can lead you to great success and profits.

A PATH TO PASSION, PURPOSE, AND PROFITS IN REAL ESTATE

Embrace your realities

A start-up's reality is bleak. Over 80% of us fail in their first few years. It doesn't matter if the odds are 80 or 95% against you, if you don't embrace the reality that today could be your last day in business, you are likely to become a statistic. The urgency and level of commitment that you must bring is hard to put into words. As an avid hockey fan, the best way to describe this notion is to watch the last 2 minutes of a Stanley Cup Game 7. I remember my partner saying to me in the first days of business that if we didn't sell $60,000 in the next month, we would have to shut down. All of a sudden, we made a sale of $120,000. Why is this?

There is a spark in all of us that we can ignite in such extreme times as we let our future reality hit us. When we find that spark we focus on our ultimate goal, work at a level of intensity that is abnormal, and tell ourselves that failure is not an option. The end result is a goal with 3 seconds left to send the game to overtime.

Some call it a miracle. I submit that it's simply true adaptability to the reality of a situation. So much of what we endured would shape our core values, which then formed our culture and identity as a company.

Ask yourself today: what are my core values as a real estate professional? What are our indispensable values as a business? In trying times, that identity can be rattled and rocked to the core many times. It's up to you to focus on making sure the foundation is solid.

Stick to your core principles

Fast-forward to summer 2007: the credit markets are falling, the sale of our company for millions of dollars falls through as a result and we are hopping on a very wild ride to say the least. Right before the Great Recession, we were a more mature company with 30 employees, making a name for ourselves in the industry.

In early 2007 the phone was ringing with new opportunity almost every day. All of a sudden, we couldn't get some of our best clients on the phone. Times like these test your relationships and see if you'll stick to your core principles or make it through the storm.

If you've worked with us, you know we built our core culture around genuine relationships. Vendors, clients, and employees are our lifeblood and to tear the fabric of these relationships would be the beginning of the end for us. Unfortunately, many organizations use economic downturns as an excuse to abandon their core ethics and relationships, tarnishing what they've built forever.

k to your core principles when the walls around
ving in? Well, it ain't easy. For us, we started
versity and we have some great reference points
from the past to rely on. We knew when the phone would ring, it
wasn't going to be someone looking to buy all of our products but
likely a hurting client looking to get out of their contract. Rather
than stick to the law of contracts written in good times, we felt it
best to dig in with our clients and offer them some relief during
the recession, asking that they pay us back by extending their
contracts.

It was a huge success for a lot of the clients we were able to work
with. So while we made some near term sacrifices, we were also
able to improve a lot of our relationships, assets that can outlast
any recession. We were able to keep afloat for the few tough
years. More importantly, we chose not to cut any staff via layoffs.
Yes, our bonuses were smaller and holiday parties were less
extravagant, but we kept our company culture intact and dug in
together to answer the call.

I often think of where we'd be today if we followed the status
quo decisions of cutting staff, paying vendors late, and holding
our clients to every line item in their contracts. By sticking to
our core principles of business and embracing the reality of the
times we stayed nimble, we stayed proactive in current day
and we set ourselves up for a very bright future. Sure enough
in 2013, the phone is ringing again. We are hearing from those

same clients who are feeling the economy changing, the credit markets thawing, foreclosures reducing and a bright outlook for the market.

During the recessions we fought through, we lost some great clients and wore out some great employees. In no way am I writing this from my soapbox. We all learned some very valuable lessons – some the hard way. In the end, our core stayed solid and we molded a new ball of clay around it to adapt to the turbulent and unpredictable times.

Embrace your new realities

As I write this, the sun shines again. The stock market is up, unemployment is down, and reports from economists are now bullish on the real estate industry. Part of the excitement of the upswing is realizing that things aren't going back to the way they were. Recessions change landscapes, they change thinking and they require a tremendous amount of adaptability to yield an optimal outcome. People may be investing again, but the path to ROI is shorter than ever.

For your business, consider: can you bring a greater intensity to your mission every day, even in good times? Could you do more with less?

Adaptability shouldn't teach us to live in fear and be too safe. We should simply embrace the new realities of our times and formulate our business strategies around them. For me, it was as simple as never forgetting where I came from and staying true to what got me here in the first place.

LIVING
THE GOOD LIFE

Krisstina Wise
CEO, The Goodlife Team
@krisstinawise

When considering what I would tell a new agent or even my own child, embarking on a life-long career in real estate, I realized I needed to give my answer in two parts.

I'd like to start by talking about what I think an agent's big-picture philosophy should always be, because I think everything flows out of the top-level philosophy of any entity, whether it's a brand, a brokerage, a team or even an individual agent. Then I want to move on and talk more specifically about how this aligns with a huge passion of mine: customer experience.

Regarding the first point, top-level philosophy, here are my thoughts:

Speak and act with authenticity and integrity. Be real, say what you mean and mean what you say. Authenticity is really, truly important.

Take personal responsibility for your actions, which includes being accountable for your failures and giving credit where credit is due.

Not everyone will necessarily agree with this, but I believe that we cannot succeed alone and that only powerful teams can produce greatness, no matter the size. The job has become too complicated for any one person to do on their own. The days of the "Lone Ranger" agent are over.

Accept that every action produces a consequence. This means you need to be aware of the potential consequences your actions will produce, and you must act to produce the intended outcomes you seek. Things don't happen by accident. Make the right things happen via your specific intentions and actions.

While being service oriented is supremely important - and in fact that's the focus of the second part of what I'm going to share here - you need to also focus on the profitability of your business. The hard reality is that you can't live a good life without the financial resources to pay for it.

Secondly, I believe in living a good life. I further believe that you achieve a good life by "producing" it. A good life to me is about a successful career, meaningful relationships with family and friends, and living a healthy and happy life. This doesn't happen passively. We produce it via the quality of our character, the quality of our work and the quality of the people we surround ourselves with. We live a good life to helping others live their good lives, too.

Drive and embrace change, creative thinking and innovation. Focus on what is best for your customers and make whatever changes are necessary to benefit them. Do not get stuck in any process that has lost its value.

Enjoy the journey and incorporate fun into what you do. It's so easy to get sucked into the vortex of workaholism and focusing on nothing but the money. If you're not enjoying your career, you're probably doing the wrong thing (or maybe working in the wrong place). When we have a closing in our office, we do something we call "ring the rooster." It's a celebration of success and happiness. And it's just fun.

Always be becoming a better version of yourself. This means you should seek out new and specialized knowledge enabling you to become expert in certain areas. As real estate becomes more and more complex, you should seek to master a few things, rather than be average at everything (that's why the team concept is so important).

Hold moods of passion, optimism and curiosity. Moods are contagious, and we spread our moods to others, whether we realize it or not. Do not contaminate your environment with bad moods. Always seek to live in moods of ambition, humility, seriousness, rigor, curiosity, wonder, enthusiasm and have a passion for life, career and business.

A healthy body equals a healthy mind. Here's an interesting fact about life: we can't go anywhere or do anything without our bodies. This means our physical, emotional and spiritual health are important for our success and accomplishment. You ultimately take care of others by taking care of yourself first. With those big picture thoughts out of the way, I'm now going to move on to customer experience, which is my ultimate passion in this industry.

As we grew up, most of us heard about the Golden Rule: "do unto others as you would have them do unto you." Or maybe your lesson was about karma. The belief is in cause and effect, that what we put out into the universe comes back to us, whether it's positive or negative. So how might these life lessons with which most of us are familiar translate into something we can consciously apply to the real estate industry and our business?

I can share how I did it my business. When I started GoodLife Team in 2008, I incorporated specific beliefs - which we call our core values - into the concept. And one of our six core values states that we always provide a "five-star" customer experience for our clients. And we do this because making sure our clients live their good life, in turn, helps us achieve our good life (which we call "GoodLife" inside our culture; obviously, we believe in this so much it's what we named the company).

But let me back up a little bit, and tell you how I came to the realization that this was something I wanted to include in my business and build into the very DNA of our organization.

First, it's important to note that I was a high-producing real estate agent for many years before I started my own company. In fact, I ran one of the highest-producing teams for a major brand in Austin, Texas, and we performed at the pinnacle of our market for a number of years. And after a few years of enjoying that level of success, I realized that what drove me, what ultimately allowed me to achieve that level of success and what really set me apart from other agents was one primary thing: the customer experience that I provided to my clients.

Once I decided to break away from that big-box brokerage and start my own real estate company, I knew that I wanted this new company to be known for providing each and every client a legitimate five-star customer experience. That was job one, priority one and my ultimate ambition. Five. Star. Experience. Period.

To help you better understand what a great customer experience entails, let's consider my five favorite brands. These were the brands I analyzed back when I was putting the finishing touches on our company concept:

Apple
Zappos
Starbucks
JetBlue
Four Seasons

At first, my impression of these companies was that Starbucks sold coffee, Zappos sold shoes, Apple sold kick-ass products, JetBlue sold seats and Four Seasons sold a night's stay. But then I had my "big aha" moment, which was this: what these companies are all selling is not really a product or service so much as a great experience for their customers.

You might have noticed that I didn't say that these companies claim to be "customer service companies." They claim to be "customer experience companies." And that begs this question: is that just a superficial difference in semantics, or is there a real difference between "customer service" and "customer experience?"

What I have come to realize is that we are now in an experience economy. Most people living in America have all of their basic needs met: food, shelter, transportation, etc. What many now prefer to spend their money on is an experience.

They buy Apple products not just because they are reputable, innovative instruments of technology, but because Apple has brilliantly created something more than just a "computer store." It's a combination of style, design, atmosphere, a "Genius Bar" staffed by people who are amazingly knowledgeable and so much more. Apple has created a culture that really appeals to a lot of people (it's the brand of computer we use at my company). You can walk into almost any mall in America, at any time of day or night, and one store will be full or nearly full and buzzing with activity: the Apple store.

And Zappos has become famous for "delivering happiness." The founder - Tony Hsieh - has written a best-selling book about his building that company, and people flock to take guided tours of their facility in Las Vegas. Talk about an "experience!"

And people pay very high prices and frequently wait in very long lines for Starbucks coffee. Because it's more than coffee. It's a meeting place, a co-working space and a place with a unique vibe that is all its own. Again, it's a palpable experience, not just a pricey cup of java.

And so on. You get the gist. All of these companies I studied had this similar "extra wow" factor that allowed them to perform better than their competition.

Each of the brands declares themselves to be a "customer experience company." And I believe that they are (and I have a basis for that opinion, as I am a customer of every one of these brands for that very reason). They claim that what makes their products/services amazing is their commitment to and standards for providing the FULL customer experience.

And is a commitment to a great customer experience that different from a person's commitment to go out every day and make a difference in someone's life? To treat someone as they would want be treated? To put a positive experience out in the universe so it comes back to them somewhere down the road?

I think they are one and the same, don't you?

Bringing this back to what we've done at GoodLife Team, here's the core value that exists in our annual strategic plan:

> "Deliver 'Wow' through service. We exist to take care of our clients. Our choices revolve around what is in their best interest. By surpassing the industry benchmark for service we strive to produce a "wow" experience for every client. A wow experience means that the client receives an "uncommon" experience from the first phone call through the successful completion of the real estate transaction. We are structured as a team for this reason: to take care of every part of their transaction with the greatest of care and competency."

All that said, I'll leave you with this: the single most valuable thing you can have in a real estate career - other than integrity and a great reputation, of course - is the ability to consistently deliver a "five-star" experience to every client.

Ask yourself this one question: What did I do TODAY to deliver that five-star experience to my clients? If you keep asking yourself that question, day after day after day, and you seek to honestly fulfill on all that that implies, you'll have more success than you need. Of that, I am very confident.

A TALE OF FAILURE AND SUCCESS

Kendyl Young
Owner, Diggs
@kendyl

I spent 25 years convinced that I would never, NEVER, create my own real estate company.

I had a lot of reasons for that belief, but it all boiled to one huge factor. I was afraid. Afraid of failure, of success, of heartbreak, of disappointment. I was afraid I would change into a person unrecognizable to my friends and family, that I would become the evil business woman caricature of the 80s, fabulously wealthy, but hideously wrinkled in spirit, character, and soul. Mostly, though, I was afraid to step into my light.

"Our deepest fear is not that we are inadequate. Our deepest fear is that we are powerful beyond measure. It is our light, not our darkness that most frightens us. We ask ourselves, Who am I to be brilliant, gorgeous, talented, fabulous?" – Marianne Williamson

Who am I, indeed? Do you ever feel this way? Do you shrink from your greatness? Do you find comfort in playing small? Do you feel that, at some level, you do not deserve to be the fabulous human being God intended you to be?

The rest of the quote gets me, every time:

> "Actually, who are you not to be? You are a child of God. Your playing small does not serve the world. There is nothing enlightened about shrinking so that other people won't feel insecure around you. We are all meant to shine, as children do. We were born to make manifest the glory of God that is within us. It's not just in some of us; it's in everyone. And as we let our own light shine, we unconsciously give other people permission to do the same. As we are liberated from our own fear, our presence automatically liberates others."
>
> Marianne Williamson

It is time to let the light shine. As I am writing this, I am at the very beginning stages of launching my own real estate brand, DIGGS. It is the first step toward creating an entire company. I am scared to death and it is easily the best thing I have ever done in my professional life.

To understand how I was able to grow my belief, and the lessons I learned, it is helpful to understand a little bit about my journey.

I am the daughter of a "force of nature, defines professionalism, household name" real estate agent. To say I had a hard time finding and filling my own shoes is a bit of an understatement!

You are not the result of a single influence or person.

You're the sum total of your life experiences plus your conscious choice of who you want to be. You choose. It's not forced upon you.

I started my real estate career when it became clear that I was not employee material, approximately six months into my first job out of college. I worked for a humongous Fortune 100 consumer goods company and I didn't believe in the mission (sell cake mix), couldn't understand the point of daily reports, and I spoke my mind- frequently and unedited.

I did everything I could think of to fit in, including some truly heinous medium blue suits and a botched attempt at drinking cocktails, but nothing seemed to work. The best thing I ever did was stop trying and find something else.

Do not put lipstick on a pig.

If you don't fit, don't change yourself, change your situation.

I had the complete advantage of starting in real estate when I was young and innocent. I knew hard work and long hours were required, but I had no concept of failure. If there was an opportunity- answer phones, sit open house, write an article, show a house- I did it with no question of whether or not I was ready or likely to succeed.

Did I fail and make mistakes? You bet! But it isn't the mistakes I remember 26 years later. It is the ways my naiveté led to spectacular wins. The first offer I wrote, cribbing from the sample contract right in front of my buyer, yet winning in an 18-offer battle. The For Sale By Owner listing—I called to see if I could show it to my buyer and then asked if I could interview for the listing because my training manual said to ask. I got the appointment, and the listing, and the malicious jealousy of most of the agents in my office who had also interviewed for the listing.

Don't wait to be ready

That will never happen. Act as if you have it all together, and, faster than you would believe, you will. Your mistakes will fade, but your gains will create the person you were meant to be.

I sold homes for seven years in the Silicon Valley. During that time my husband quit his job and became my support crew. It was the best thing we could have done, and it is a job he excels at to this day.

How did we work together as partners and as husband and wife?

An early mentor taught us the dangers of Hat Confusion. "Hats" are a good way to visualize roles, and hat clarity is the key to smooth communications. For example, in a money conversation, am I wearing the Wife Hat or the Head of Business Hat? Does he answer as Head of Family or as Support Crew? If our "hats" are misaligned, tension and misunderstanding ensue.

Understand the different roles or "hats" that exist in your relationships

We enjoyed a lot of success in Silicon Valley, but when we were ready to start a family I had to go back home. Being far from family, once we had started our own, was not an option. We sold everything, moved to Glendale, and started all over again, from scratch and six months pregnant. In the middle of a recession.

Know your priorities in life

My priority was family over success and money. Restarting my real estate career was an adventure in self identity. I had been a Super Star and a Big Shot in Silicon Valley. In Glendale, I was Bea Jue's pregnant daughter who was "getting into" real estate. That

I looked like a 16 year old, on a good day, did not help. That my mother was a real estate icon and hyper competitive did not help.

It was amazing how people defined me as an extension of my mother. It was even more amazing how much I bought into that same identity. I saw myself as a protege who would certainly be a great star someday, but whose time had not yet come. In hindsight, I realize that I was the only one putting myself in that box.

You are always in control of your box

You can tell yourself any story you want, and your mind will accept it as reality. Why tell yourself a crappy story?

Over the next few years I enjoyed reasonable success. I was comfortably in the middle of the pack and I wasn't rocking any boats. My mother, always a "believer", decided that we should sign up for a coaching program. It absolutely changed my life.

A good coach will challenge your beliefs and your stories. They will encourage you to identify your "why" and they help you find a path toward realizing it.

A great coach will identify and call you out on your BS and blow apart your excuses. A great coach holds you absolutely accountable and instills an unshakable belief that anything is possible.

I started with a good coach and doubled my business, twice. I wound up with a great coach, Steve Shull, and doubled my life, several times over.

With Steve, I learned how I was holding myself back. I learned how to take responsibility, how to dream big and how to believe in my greatness. Could I have grown this much without his guidance? Possibly, but it would take far, far longer.

A coach is invaluable

You can't see the roadblocks you set up for yourself, but your coach can. The sooner you get a great coach, the sooner you will fill your greatness.

In 2005, I realized that I was bored. I am a learning junkie and I love to acquire new skills and experiences. Selling lots of homes was uninspiring.

Fortunately, it was right about this time that the internet started to influence the behaviors of the home buyers and sellers. I realized that the internet would go far beyond simply letting the public shop for homes without an agent. I saw that it would fundamentally change the way customers would make decisions and how they would relate to their agents. If agents are not the gatekeeper of the listing information, what would our role become? I could not have been more excited, and I immediately started a blog and set out to learn all I could about the changing expectations of the buying and selling public.

Embrace change, because change is life

Almost everyone else is running from change or denying that it's happening. There is great advantage and opportunity for those who recognize, and leverage, this basic fact of life.

Facebook became a huge part of my professional life in 2011. For the first time I was in an environment where I wasn't the crazy idealist. I found other agents, company owners, and consultants who recognized the real estate industry had massive potential for change and were passionate about finding a better way. Many of these people were smarter, more accomplished, and had fancier titles than I did, but it didn't matter. I learned from them, exchanged ideas, and realized that I had valid and valuable ideas of my own. Because of them, I learned to see myself in a new light.

You are who you associate with

Choose your associates as carefully as you would choose your children's friends.

And, here we are, back to the present. I have accomplished more than I thought possible and I am on the cusp of a grand, new, adventure. This is the year that I turn 50 and I have to say that I can't wait to see what the next 50 years will bring!

FORWARD

"One does not accumulate
but eliminate. It is not daily
increase but daily decrease.
The height of cultivation
always runs to simplicity."

— **Bruce Lee**

REAL PATH - IT'S ALL CONNECTED

"A lobster when left high and dry among the rocks, has not the instinct and energy enough to work his way back to the sea, but waits for the sea to come to him. If it does not come, he remains where he is and dies, although the slightest effort would enable him to reach the waves, which are perhaps within a yard of him.

The world is FULL of Human Lobsters: Men stranded on the rocks of indecision and procrastination, who instead of putting forth their own energies are waiting for some Grand Billow of good fortune to set them afloat."
– Dr. Orrison Swett Marden

While I'm a strong advocate of positive thinking and mindfulness, happy day dreams are not the same as work. Progress is only possible with change; change is made possible with action. Movement is life.

What stalls most progress is the misconception (thus fear) that getting from point A to point B requires more energy, skill, and time than you have. But the truth is that big problems are rarely solved with big solutions. Instead, dilemmas are solved via a sequence of small, incremental steps, made over days, weeks, months, or even years.

Consider, for instance, losing weight. Dropping forty pounds occurs ounce-by-ounce. Each reduction is hardly dramatic, but the end result is. A small daily effort yields a big payoff after some number of weeks.

Here's another example. When I was 22, I went skydiving with some friends. We took a four-hour class to prepare, where some training was spent reviewing procedures, but most focused on positioning our bodies. Form — something akin to the top of a jumping jack, legs slightly spread, arms raised, and hands near your head — is key to a stable free fall.

After ground school, we boarded a one-seater, single-engine plane with two instructors. It was a cheap, old plane, with exposed metal interior, and we sat on the floor, sans seat belts, for the 30-minute ride to an altitude of 10,000 feet. When the pilot indicated "Go!," the instructor flung the door open, unleashing a veritable hurricane inside the cramped quarters. For first timers, this is when fear mercilessly grabs you by the throat.

Worse, this was not a "jump out the door" sort of skydive. Preparing to jump required the three of us to climb out of the plane and hold onto the bar that supports the overhead wing. Well, literally, it means dangling off the side of an airplane. Once set up, with the instructors hanging on to each side of me, we all let go.

After five or so seconds of tumbling, not knowing which way is up and which is down, we stabilized by forming the "jumping jack" position. The sensation of falling subsided, replaced by a feeling of flying. It's truly wonderful.

However, small movements matter. A lot. If you move one hand just a few inches without countering with the other hand, you start spinning. If you angle a foot without adjusting the other, you lose control. Careening out of the sky made physical what I had always perceived: small things add up. Everything is connected.

Subtle changes affect business and life, too, even if not felt immediately. As in skydiving, movement should be intentional. Most people tend to focus on the one hundred things they should do. But too much action with too little intent confuses movement for progress.

I learned to focus on the three to eight things required to accomplish an objective. I don't get distracted by the ninety two other (seemingly important) things that ultimately don't contribute to personal growth or the success of my company.

I call my approach the "Real Path."

"Real" reflects that the approach is practical, aimed at achieving goals. "Real" also indicates that the method is realistic: It's likely you'll have to tweak and evolve yourself and your business along the way. Finally, "Real" is apt because it captures the effects of the real world. Everything is connected and small changes in one area can have positive/negative effects on another.

I've identified seven interrelated components key to running a business with purpose, passion, and profits. Those areas are *People, Value, Habits, Organization, Health, Mind, Rejuvenation, and Growth.*

PEOPLE - COMPOUNDED INTEREST

*"Compound interest is the eighth wonder of the world.
He who understands it, earns it, he who doesn't, pays it."*
– Albert Einstein

Compound interest arises when interest is added to the principal, so that, from that moment on, the interest that has been added also earns interest. This addition of interest to the principal is called compounding.

While not everyone takes advantage of compound interest, this is universal knowledge. But what most business people don't pay attention to is the compounded interest of the ACTIONS they take everyday – nor the compound interest of the PEOPLE they have relationships with.

That's how we came up with our minimalist approach to building your People Portfolio. Think of it as a simple 3x3 - meet three people face to face, every day.

- Contact them three times over three weeks (the first meeting counts as contact).

- The objective is to add three people to your Portfolio weekly.

- This simple strategy has compounded effects on your business, just as every leg or arm movement does while falling from 12,000 feet above the Earth.

Three people per week adds up to 150 people in your database per year. At the end of three years, you'll have approximately 450 people in your People Portfolio – and if nurtured as we have recommend, will equal roughly 30-60 transactions per year just from your people base.

At the end of ten years you'll have 1,000-1,500 people in your database. Now that is a sustainable business.

Compounded action pays BIG dividends

One of the things I've learned in my last seven years of creating new habits is the power of compound action interest. It sounds really obvious when you say it, but if you do something small repeatedly, the benefits accrue greatly over time. It's obvious, but not everyone puts it into practice.

Here's how to create action investments. It's a fairly simple process that you can repeat with any of these various types of action investments:

1. Pick something desirable like meeting new people. If you repeatedly do this activity, what will it grow into? Is that what you want?

2. Do just 20-30 minutes of it per day. You can't build it all up in the next few days (that's a good recipe for failure). Do it in short spurts and smile as you do it.

3. Set a daily reminder. Let's say you want to do this task every day at 10:30 a.m. Set a reminder, and make it a priority to do it each day, just for five minutes.

4. Watch it grow. If you just do it repeatedly, it will grow. Don't force it. Keep the repeated activity as small as possible for as long as you can if you want it to grow (it sounds paradoxical, but it works).

A few warnings:

- Don't worry about doing a lot of it. As you repeat this new habit, don't worry about growing it. That's a good way to fail. Most people fail at adopting new behaviors because they try to do too much too quickly.

- Don't worry about missing a day or two. This is another reason people fail — they miss a day or two, then just give up. If you miss a day or two (or three), just start again. It doesn't have to be a big deal.
- Don't do a bunch at a time. Do one per day at the most. Remember, small time chunks.

You're making daily deposits, tiny investments in who you are. What do you want to invest in? Can you make tiny contributions to your People Portfolio? Health? Value? Growth? Infrastructure?

Getting the point? You can invest in something that will grow your business and enhance your life in small ways that add to big interest, or it can be a life of distraction and bad health. It doesn't take Warren Buffett to decide what is a better investment.

VALUE - MARKETING THAT LASTS

*"Don't ask what the world needs.
Ask what makes you come alive, and go do it.
Because what the world needs
is people who have come alive."*
– Howard Thurman

It's estimated that most people see tens of thousands of marketing messages a day, and you might see even more than that, depending on where you live in the world. That's a lot of messages. And most of them are trying to convince you of something.

Marketing is neither good nor bad. It is simply the way a company speaks to us. People use their mouths, companies use marketing. It is subjective. However, *how* companies choose to speak to us is another story. And in that case, how they market to us is mostly bad.

- o   Good marketing speaks **for** us.
- o   Bad marketing speaks **at** us.

- Good marketing starts with **a cause.**
- Bad marketing starts with **a goal.**

- Good marketing drives **loyalty.**
- Bad marketing drives **transactions.**

- Good marketing **promotes values.**
- Bad marketing **values promotions.**

- Good marketing tells us exactly **what a company really thinks.**
- Bad marketing tells us **what the company thinks they want us to think they think.**

- Good marketing **seduces.**
- Bad marketing **targets.**

- Good marketing **never mentions commission rates.**
- Bad marketing **always does.**

- Good marketing uses clients and services to **help tell a story.**
- Bad marketing **tells stories about themselves.**

- Good marketing is about **us.**
- Bad marketing is about **them.**

- Bad marketing **manipulates.**
- Good marketing **inspires.**

Less Marketing – More Creating

The shift that has occurred because of social media is marketing from a megaphone (mass email, advertising, canned messages) to a position of being able to simply LISTEN. Clients are sharing how their lives are unfolding on Facebook, Twitter, LinkedIn, and others, providing endless opportunities to communicate with meaning and authenticity. Let go of a social media 'strategy or tactic' and use tools that help you listen to your people base and communicate with them in the various layers (SMS text, email, tweets, FB), but always keep communications REAL. Remember the saying: Seek not to be understood... but to understand.

We are an industry of small business, paradoxically adopting the poor behavior and bad habits of big box brands. My advice: *embrace* being small, because big business can't copy authentic one-on-one relationships. These relationships are the only path to building a sustainable real estate business, but it is what the industry struggles with the most.

The purpose of marketing is to get to a level of depth with your people base, where traditional marketing is no longer required and is replaced instead with authentic communication. I've spent hundreds of thousands in marketing and advertising. It's a viscous cycle with no end, and one you can break with authenticity.

HABITS - WHAT TIME FAVORS MOST

"The definition of insanity is doing the same thing over and over again and expecting different results."
– Albert Einstein

Einstein was right...doing the same thing over and over again and expecting a different result - like making new year resolutions or a long list of goals - is a sure fire way to drive yourself nuts and beat yourself up the following November or December when you reflect back on your year. I've done it for the better part of 15 years, and it got me nowhere. Resolutions are pipe-dreams, and goals if not backed by habits, are as effective as wishing-upon-a-star - they are designed to make you feel busy, or that you're being effective and that all you need to turn things around, is have a plan.

Life is chaotic, busy, random, and quite frankly, fleeting, passing most people by while they're thinking about it. For most of us, sticking with big plans for a few weeks is highly unlikely, let alone sticking to them for an entire year. So what do you do to turn things around and improve your life? By taking control of the only thing you can: Your day.

"We are what we repeatedly do.
Excellence, then, is not an act, but a habit"
– Aristotle

The Pointlessness of Plans

Many of the best things in life happen with no plan or goal attached, as they tend to happen on their own. Life has a way of rewarding action and intention: Falling in love, friendships, a new client out of the blue, etc.

If you want to make the weeks, months, and years to come count, you'll need to be intentional — not by setting goals, but by adopting the right daily habits that set the stage of you being the best you. It sounds cheesy, but stick with me.

By focusing on incremental changes in the form of daily habits, I was able to lose 50lbs, launch a new company, run a half-marathon (when I hadn't run a mile in 20 years), get stronger than I have ever been in my life, and take my family on the adventure of moving to another state, all while loving every minute of it and without the formula of a broad plan.

I just finished one of the best years of my life, and most of it was completely unplanned. How, you ask? By creating new disciplines I actually liked doing. I wasn't only fixated on the end results – I also enjoyed the process.

This is the secret to a healthy, productive life and to making an impact on the world, even through your career. Create good, sustainable habits that you enjoy, and you'll end up with a life you can be proud of, a real estate business that becomes sustainable and income predictable.

"Psychology research tells us that the average amount of time necessary to reach 'maximum automacity' (a habit) is 66 days. But when you are trying to develop a healthy habit, it's likely it will take 80 days for it to become automatic. The more complex the habit, the longer it takes to form." -David DiSalvo

For me, it takes roughly 80 days to adopt a habit through consistency and moderation, but this is a round number and will vary from person to person and habit to habit. Often you'll read a magical "21 days" to change a habit, but this is a myth not based on any scientific evidence.

Although DiSalvo says the average is 66 days, I recommend 30 days as a good number to get started as it's not overwhelming and can be accomplished by anyone. Your challenge: stick with a habit every day for 30 days and post your daily progress updates to a journal.

> *"Time is the friend of the wonderful habits,*
> *the enemy of the mediocre ones."*
> – Warren Buffett

Focus on just one habit at a time

This is important. As simple as it sounds, even changing just one habit is not easy. Resist the temptation to list 50 things you want to change about yourself or new habits you want to adopt - trust me, start slow or you're setting yourself up for failure. Keep it simple, and allow yourself to focus and be accountable. Here are some ideas you may want to start with:

Get up early. I get up around five every morning - when there are the least distractions possible. If you are going to focus on creating a sustainable real estate business, you'll need to find the time. The best way to do this is to start while others are sleeping. At first, I didn't like waking up before the sun, but eventually my body adjusted and I began looking forward to the solitude and loved that my email inbox didn't fill up before my eyes, so I was able to actually focus.

Get fit. Our bodies are not like a car one can simply trade-in. We have one body, one sole means of functioning. Fit bodies lead to better health, confidence, and more success. There is no such thing as not having enough time during the day. Getting fit actually creates time.

Stop making "sales" and focus on one new connection a day

Forging new relationships makes the world go round. When you meet new people, you make connections that can lead to all kinds of future breakthroughs. Stop trying to "sell" people on using your services, rather focus on forging a relationship and providing value to that relationship. Even when it's uncomfortable, reach out and introduce yourself to new people...try knocking on 100 doors a day and simple say "Hi, I'm Dave. I'm a broker with XYZ. I wanted to meet you face to face and wondered if you'd mind if I emailed you recent real estate activity on occasion?" The worst they can say is "no." Fortunately, many won't.

Start small

Because habit change is challenging and trying to take on too much is a guaranteed recipe for disaster, the smaller the better. Want to get fit? Start with a 5-10 daily minute walk. Want to wake up earlier? Try just ten minutes earlier for now. Want to make new connections? Try just knocking on ten doors a day.

The best year of your life is within reach — if you are willing to give up on the crazy unpredictability of plans and instead focus on creating new habits.

ORGANIZING FOR THE DISORGANIZED

It is often said that if you want to really know a person, go to their home and open their drawers or closet. Many people are outwardly clean and organized, but the true measure of someone's life is their drawers – are they stuffed full of knick knacks or are they tidy? The answer is telling.

You're probably rolling your eyes right now, because like most people, you shove things in drawers without a second thought. We implore you to stop. Keeping your surroundings clear can help unclutter your mind, and help you focus on your purpose.

When you wake up in the morning, what is the first thing you see? Do you roll over to see piles of laundry, a layer of dust, and a stack of magazines by your bedside? Are you haunted by the fact that there are dishes from last night still in the sink and there are bicycles on the front lawn?

Before you end your day, tidy up. It's simple – take ten minutes before you leave your office to straighten and put away any last files or books, and take ten minutes before bed time to put the throw pillows on the couch in the upright position.

The funny thing is that once you adopt this policy for yourself, it will spill over into other parts of your life – you'll begin actually deleting emails and voicemails rather than letting them pile up, you'll slowly begin meeting deadlines and using your tech tools more effectively.

Additionally, keeping your surroundings clear helps avoid overwhelming your brain activity, as our brains are designed to constantly take in the billions of data points around us, and keeping calm in your visible environment can go a long way toward being productive and promotes better mental health overall.

We're not saying you should somehow try to become OCD and scrub your phone every day, we're saying that even though your dirty desk is okay with you, your brain is actually digesting the data and barricading function, not to mention clients often look at it as a sign that you don't tend to the details.

Ten minutes a day can make all of your other new habits infinitely easier to accomplish because you're focused. It doesn't have to be complicated.

HEALTH -
SUSTAINABLY YOU

As you've probably noticed by now, we take sustainability seriously. We have one body, one vehicle to get through life with and we need to take care of our human capital so we're not exhausted, sleep deprived, and burned out. It's not going to do you any good to work on building a business for a few years... and then get sick without being able to enjoy it. We want you healthy and the least we can do is illustrate the basics for that.

This is not about vanity. It's about sustainability. If that's not enough, a recent study[1] found that people who exercise earn on average 9% more than those who don't. On the flip side, in a 2007 study[2], those who were technically obese earned on average of 18% less than those who weren't.

A growing body of evidence suggests we think and learn better when we walk or do another form of exercise, as exercise enhances cognition due to improved blood flow. Research shows that when we exercise, blood pressure and blood flow increase everywhere in the body, including the brain. More blood means more energy and oxygen, which makes our brain perform better.

We know... this is bizarre. What kind of book on real estate is this, talking about health? We've heard it before... and we're not here to preach, but we do take this seriously and we live it ourselves. We're not talking about your becoming an elite athlete, rather establishing a good baseline in order to build the strongest, leanest, healthiest body possible, taking clues from evolutionary biology.

Sometimes we get so lost in building our business and living life that we just can't see the forest through the trees. We overlook the simplicity and ease with which we could all be achieving exceptional health and fitness – which has a proven direct effect on energy, inspiration, and yes, income.

We do the same thing in business... we look for the quick fixes, when the best solution is dedication and hard work. This chapter may not be for everyone, but we've been on the journey, have performed years of research and experiments for the best and simplest solutions. And here are 10 simple guidelines we recommend learned from Mark Sisson creator of the Primal Blueprint:

Our Disclaimer: Please don't be stupid and overdo any of this. It would make us quite unhappy. Consult a doctor before doing anything in this book.

Eat lots of animals and plants

I don't want to offend or condescend to vegetarians or vegans. We respect choice. However, humans are omnivores, after all.

That said, not all meat is created equal. Focus on quality sources of protein (all forms of meat, fowl, fish ideally from sources that allow animals to graze in natural environments – example, grass-fed beef vs feed lots), lots of colorful vegetables, some select fruits (mostly berries), and healthy fats (nuts, avocados, olive oil). Observe portion control (80% of fullness) unless you are performing rigorous exercise with massive calorie output. Eliminate grains, sugars, trans- and hydrogenated fats from your diet.

Move around a lot at a slow pace

As real estate agents, we tend to sit at our desks a lot. This is not healthy and researchers agree that it has similar long term health consequences as smoking. So commit to doing some form of low level aerobic activity 2-5 hours a week, whether it is walking, hiking, easy bike riding or swimming.

Lift heavy things

We're not suggesting you need to become an Olympic lifter, but if you're able, go to the gym and lift weights two to three times a week. Ditch the machines and focus on movements that involve the entire body and in wider ranges of motion. Emulate the movements of our ancestors: jumping, squatting, lunging, pushing, pulling, twisting, etc. This will stimulate your genes to increase muscle strength and power, increase bone density, improve insulin sensitivity, stimulate growth hormone secretion, and consume stored body fat – not to mention, it's an incredible natural reliever of stress.

Run really quickly every once in a while

When is the last time you ran as fast as you could (without being chased)? Do some form of intense anaerobic sprint bursts a couple times a week. This could be as simple as six or eight (or more) short sprints up a hill, on the grass, at the beach... or repeated intense sessions on a bicycle (stationary, road or mountain bike). These short bursts also increase human growth hormone (HGH) release, which is actually released in proportion to the intensity (not the duration) of the exercise.

Get lots of sleep

Get plenty of quality sleep. Our lives are so hectic and full of things to do after the sun goes down that it's often difficult to get an adequate amount of sleep. Yet sleep is one of the most important factors in maintaining good health, vibrant energy, and a strong immune system.

Play

Spend some time each week involved in active play. In addition to allowing you to apply your fitness to a real-life situation, play helps dissipate some of the negative effects of the chronic stress hormones you've been accumulating through the week.

Get some sunlight every day

Contrary to the "Common Wisdom" dispensed by dermatologists (who suggest you shun the sun), you should get some direct sunlight every day. Certainly not so much that you come close to burning, but definitely enough to prompt your body to make the all-important vitamin D and to support the mood-lifting benefits. A slight tan is a good indicator that you have maintained adequate Vitamin D levels. Natural sunlight also has a powerful mood-elevating effect, which can enhance productivity at work and in inter-personal interactions, and fresh air always does a body good.

Avoid poisonous things

We all have busy days and when time is tight, it's all too tempting to hit the drive thru at a fast food joint to get some calories in. Please don't. The things we eat either add to or take away from our health. All it takes is a little planning. Try shopping on the perimeter of the grocery store. Most of what is healthful is on the outskirts (fruits, veggies, meat). Avoid fast and processed food and also try to avoid the hidden poisons in foods like sugars, grains, processed foods, trans and hydrogenated fats, and mercury in certain fish.

Use your mind

Exercise your brain daily as our ancestors did. Be inventive, creative, and aware. If your work is not stimulating (or even if it is), find time to read, write, play an instrument, and interact socially.

Health and wellness have a direct effect not only on your quality of life, but also on the quality of your business. Exercising your mind and body should take precedent in your day. Continue to evolve your health routine to find out what works for you. I recommend exploring the works of Mark Sisson and Melissa & Dallas Hartwig.

Endnotes

[1] June issue of Journal of labor Research.

[2] The Economics of Obesity. GENDER, BODY MASS, AND SOCIOECONOMIC STATUS: NEWEVIDENCE FROM THE PSID.

MIND - RECLAIM YOUR BRAIN

"Reading, after a certain age, diverts the mind too much from its creative pursuits. Any man who reads too much and uses his own brain too little falls into lazy habits of thinking."
– Albert Einstein

Our brains have been changed. And not in a good way. The average person in the United States watches 2.8 hours of television every day. All told, that's 42 full, 24-hour days per year spent in front of a talking box. That's a mind-numbing statistic. And a scary trend.

Now consider how often we check Facebook, check email, search the news online, or consult our Uncle Google. It's not uncommon for workers to check their email 30-40 times *per hour* and reach for their phone at traffic lights to check Twitter or see if anyone has "liked" their status update. We've become slaves to the web, seemingly losing our ability to think and get work done.

Former *Wired* writer Nicholas Carr wrote an article titled "Is Google Making Us Stupid?" His research turned up an unsettling answer. Yes.

Indeed, the internet is changing our brains. You can sit down to look up one thing, fall down a rabbit hole of hyperlinks and related searches, and emerge an hour later, dazed and confused.

Many agents equate being at the office, hours upon hours being in front of the computer as working. It's not. And it's one of the hazards of our modern lifestyle. Our tendency to become more and more addicted to staring at screens, and more and more sedentary is unproductive at best and downright unhealthy at worst.

We look at laptops and desktop computers, iPhones and Androids and iPads and iPods, TVs and movie screens, we play video games, watch videos, surf the web, socialize online, and work online. And we're sitting the whole time. Too much screen time means less active time, less time thinking, less focus on the present, less time for getting real, productive work done, and making time for the ones you love. And too much sitting means <u>fewer years on your life</u>. So what's a better way? Limits.

Limit how much screen time you have each day. Limit the amount of time you allow yourself on the Internet (I use an application called macfreedom. It'll be the best $10 bucks you'll ever spend). Limit your sitting to short periods with breaks in between and when you must sit frequently, stand up and walk around for 10 minutes every hour.

This isn't the only way to do it — you'll have to find the limit that works for you. But the idea is to set limits, and to break the total up into pieces so you'll take breaks and do other things. I've loved it. I'm reading more books, spending more personal time with my kids, getting more chores done, and exercising more. And because you have a limit, you have to figure out the best way to use that time. You have to make choices—what's worthy of your limited time and what isn't. This means a more controlled, conscious use of your time.

I haven't instituted the limits with my kids yet, though I have been talking to them about it to get them thinking about what would work best for them. And I do tell them to take breaks from devices throughout the day so they'll do other things. For the kids, this has meant they have more unstructured, imaginative play, more reading, more art and music, more activity. Kids get addicted to screens just as much as adults do, and it's unhealthy. I'm trying to teach them ways to live a healthy lifestyle, which is a lesson with lifelong benefits.

I've found this lifestyle to be healthier, better for my relationships, and better for my peace of mind. And to me, that means it's something worth keeping and refining, because it paves the way to focus on purpose and passion.

WORK TRUE: LET GO OF THE STRESS OF MEASURING

'You can't manage what you don't measure.'
~old management adage '
You can't manage without pleasure.'
– Leo Babauta

There are a few old management adages that seem to run like a current through our society, powering our work and personal lives: "You can't manage what you don't measure" and "You are what you measure" and "Work Smart, not Hard."

But how often do we pause to ask if they're true? If you become consumed with numbers, you'll become a robot and forget the reason you're in real estate in the first place.

I've fallen for it myself. At various times, I've obsessed over tracking workouts, miles run, everything I've eaten, every single work task I complete, progress towards goals, my weight, my body fat percentage, how many days I've done a habit in a month, contacts in a day, expenses, earnings, debt, website visitors, ad clicks, tweets, followers, and on and on. Sometimes I've tracked a few of these at the same time.

And I'm not alone. There are people who track the most minute details of their lives, from heartbeats to steps walked to hours slept (and quality of the sleep) to emails sent. As a society, we're tracking and measuring more than ever before. But what's the theory here? Is it productive? Necessary?

The theory behind measuring states unless you measure something you don't know if it is getting better or worse. You can't manage for improvement if you don't measure to see what is getting better and what isn't. To some extent, this is true.

If you measure how many hours you spent prospecting, it's very possible that the number will increase simply because you are measuring it, more aware of it, more focused on it, and motivated for that number to increase. If you measure miles run, that number will likely improve (until you get injured or burnt out).

But how do you measure the good stuff? The joy, the deepening of relationships? How do you measure the great conversations you had with your client when you called to check in? How do you track the ideas you had on the run, the health benefit of the runs, the new places you explored? You could try to track all of these things, but then you'd be tracking 20 things instead of just miles run.

Work is the same way — you can measure one or 10 metrics for productivity, but does it measure the relationships you've built with your clients, or the enjoyment you've gotten doing the work, or the things you've learned by making mistakes, or the pure joy you've gotten in making someone's life better by the service you provided them? Go ahead and try to measure that.

When you track a metric, such as hours or dollars or miles, you are saying that's more important than all the things that can't be measured. You put that in the forefront of your head as the thing that must be improved, at the cost of all else. What about relationships and joy? Are those less important?

Then, there are other problems with tracking and measuring everything:

- It takes time to measure and track—that's valuable time you could have spent doing or living.

- It creates a mindset that we must always improve – and that the only way to improve is to always measure, always manage things, always strive for better, better, better (which creates a big sweaty ball of stress). What about learning to be happy with yourself? What about focusing on how awesome it is to provide value to your clients? It's stressful to measure and track a lot of things, and it's disappointing if those numbers don't go up, or don't go up as much as we'd hoped.

- We have to choose what to measure, and how do we know that we're choosing the right thing? Why is *that* thing the only one that matters? It's a narrowing way of looking at life.

- It doesn't improve happiness. It doesn't make us content. It doesn't keep us in the moment.

I could go on and on. Measurement and tracking are tools and there's nothing wrong with using them. Just consider the alternatives, question your dogma, and experiment to see what works best.

Absent tracking everything, work goes on. We work because it gives us joy and it's fulfilling to help others. Numbers lack meaning, are arbitrary, limiting, narrow, and without heart.

Do for the love of doing, for the love of others. That's immeasurable, profoundly life changing, and proven to improve your business.

REJUVENATION

"There is more to life than increasing its speed."
– Mohandas Gandhi

The mantra of our working culture is to always give 100%. It feels good to rally around such a statement – it unites us to feel like we're 'all giving our all.' But is it true? Is it realistic? Can we work 12 hour days, 7 days a week, 52 weeks a year?

I suppose we can. But should we....

The Japanese have an expression concerning healthy eating habits: *Hara hachi bu*. Hara hachi bu means "Eat until 80% full" (literally, stomach 80%). Okinawans in Japan, through practicing hara hachi bu, are the only human population to have a self-imposed habit of calorie restriction. Consequently, Okinawa has the world's highest proportion of centenarians, at approximately 50 per 100,000 people.

In a 1965 book, *Three Pillars of Zen*, the author states, "eight parts of a full stomach sustain the man; the other two sustain the doctor." The same principle can be applied to our work/life balance.

Energy and inspiration are perishable

While hara hachi bu is one simple principle that can help you have a much healthier life. It's also a principle that can be applied to the length of your work day.

Consider if a builder in your area was creating a new master planned community and offered you $5,000,000 to work for her 24 hours a day for 10 years and then retire, would you do it? Of course not – you couldn't, it's not physically possible or sustainable.

But don't most people do something similar? They often work in excess of 8 hours a day, doing the same mind-numbing motions, over and over, for 30 or 40 years – until someday they hope they have enough saved to retire (or until they have a mental or physical breakdown – which is sadly often the case).

Markets will shift, life will happen

The problem with being maxed out is you cannot deal with anything new. Running full out inhibits your adaptability when "life" happens and markets change. You simply can't fit anything else in.

It's not within our biological rhythm to have sustained energy and interest (or inspiration) for long periods of time. We need alternating periods of rest, adventure, and other activities to keep our brains and bodies fueled and inspired.

More and more of us find ourselves unable to juggle overwhelming demands and maintain a seemingly unsustainable pace. Paradoxically, the best way to get more done may be to spend more time doing less. A new and growing body of research shows that strategic renewal — including daytime workouts, short afternoon naps, longer sleep hours, more time away from the office and longer, more frequent vacations — boosts productivity, job performance and, of course, health.

"More, bigger, faster." This, the ethos of the market economies since the Industrial Revolution, is grounded in a mythical and misguided assumption — that our resources are infinite.

As mentioned earlier, vacations hold tremendous benefits for workers in any industry. In 2006, Ernst & Young performed an internal study of its employees, finding that for each additional 10 hours of vacation employees took, their year-end performance ratings from supervisors (on a scale of one to five) improved by eight percent. Frequent vacationers were also significantly less likely to leave the firm.

The importance of restoration is rooted in our physiology. Human beings aren't designed to expend energy continuously. Rather, we're meant to pulse between spending and recovering energy, whether with mental activities like our careers, or physical activities like our fitness.

Passion is fueled by loving your career, which is best done by adopting a positive attitude. We don't mean tweeting lame inspirational quotes all day or wishing for a genie to give you three wishes, no, we mean developing the habits to allow yourself to be mentally sharp, healthy, and happy.

Successful agents with this type of mentality typically take "mini-retirements" throughout their career instead of mortgaging recovery time for later in life (when there are no guarantees to get there). By working when you are most energetic and inspired, you will get more done, connect with more people at deeper levels and deliver more value to your portfolio of connections.

The energy you're able to bring to your craft is far more important in terms of the value of your work and what you create, than is the number of hours you work. By managing energy more skillfully, it's possible to get more done, in less time, more sustainably. When we're renewing, we're truly renewing, so when we're working, we can truly work.

GROWTH

*"We learn more by looking for the answer to
a question and not finding it than we do from
learning the answer itself."*
– Lloyd Alexander

When I started real estate in 1996, I didn't know how to use a computer. I could turn it on – but I didn't know Windows let alone Microsoft Word. True story.

My first colleague in real estate had a Computer Science degree and was a rocket scientist. No, seriously, he was literally a rocket scientist and real estate was his second career. His favorite line during listing appointments was "You don't have to be a rocket scientist to sell a house, but I do happen to be one."

He tasked me with making my first listing flyer on the computer and when he noticed me struggling said, 'just cut and paste'... so I printed a bunch of graphics, grabbed some scissors, and started cutting and pasting (I'm not joking).

I've made some progress since then.

- Built my own website a year later.

- Was one of first people in the market to offer password protected home search to the public (and nearly got me booted from the MLS).

- Was recruited by a dotcom in my late twenties.

- And in the end, I founded a tech company.

All because I was curious. I'm a lifelong learner and am always obsessively studying something, whether that's cooking or wine or chess or writing or fitness. We should ALWAYS continue to try new things, learn things that are foreign to us – it builds new neuropathways in the brain and keeps us young.

Here are two key lessons (both really the same lesson) I've learned about learning, in all my years of study and in trying to teach people. Almost everything I've learned, I didn't learn in school; and almost everything I've learned, and everything most kids have learned, we've all learned on their own.

*"The only thing that interferes
with my learning is my education."*
– Albert Einstein

This is part of your work. Being a successful real estate artisan requires that you continue to evolve, to learn, to grow so you can deepen relationships and provide ongoing value to your friends, family, and your portfolio.

PRACTICE

"Everything is practice."
— Pele

When we learn to ride a bike, surf, ski, or throw a ball, we practice these movements in a deliberate way, we practice it consciously and repeatedly. Through conscious and repeated practice, we become good at those movements.

If we take a moment to pause, we'll see that nearly every moment of our day is practice - from waking up, how we answer calls, how we give listing presentations - our entire lives are like this, but we're often less 'conscious' of the practice.

Each day, we repeat movements, thought patterns, ways of interacting with others ... and in this repeated practice, we are becoming (or have already become) good at these things. If you constantly check Facebook or Twitter, that is practice, and you are forming that habit, though it's usually subconscious.

When you get frustrated with other agents, the market conditions, or put yourself down internally, this is something you are practicing. You may already be good at these things.

What if, instead, we practiced consciously, deliberately, and became good at the things we really want to be good at?

What if you first, above all skills, learned to be more aware of what you are practicing? What if constant conscious action is the skill you became good at?

If you could learn to take conscious action, you could learn to practice other things you want to be good at, rather than the ones you don't.

What are you practicing?

Ask yourself these things throughout the day, to practice conscious action:

- Do I want to practice rushing through my morning, or can I wake a little earlier and simplify my morning routine so that I practice a paced, enjoyable morning ritual?

- Do I want to practice checking my inboxes when I first get to my computer, or can I do something better like write a blog or journal?

- Do I want to practice complaining about the market, or do I want to practice connecting with people in my community?

- Do I want to practice rushing communicating with new and past clients, or do I want to practice listening and deepening my relationship with them?

- Do I want to practice eating fried foods, sugary foods, salty junk food snacks, fast foods, or can I practice eating whole foods, vegetables and fruits, nuts and beans and seeds?

- Do I want to practice surfing time-wasting sites or can I practice clearing away distractions and creating?

- Do I want to practice watching mindless entertainment or can I practice moving my body and exerting myself in activity?

These are only examples... your life will show you what you've been practicing, and you can decide what you would rather practice instead. Or, you might find that you are completely happy with what you've been practicing.

How to practice

The first step is always awareness. When you are conscious of what you are doing, you can decide whether this is an action or thought pattern you want to practice, or if there's an alternative you'd rather be good at.

As you go through your day, practice this awareness. It's the first skill, and it's the most important one. Without feeling guilty or angry at yourself, be aware of what you're doing and thinking. You will forget to do this, but remind yourself. You might wear a rubber band around your wrist and snap it when you catch yourself in a practice you'd like to change.

As you become good at conscious action, start to practice those actions and thought patterns you want to be good at. Start to notice the ones you'd really rather not be good at, and see if you can deliberately practice other actions and thought patterns.

As you consciously, deliberately repeat these things, you'll get better at them. It takes a lot of repetition to get good at a skill, but you've got time.

"I'm such a good lover because I practice a lot on my own."
– Woody Allen
(Come on. We had to add some humor.)

CASE STUDY

Profile:	Bill Watson
Market:	Phoenix Metro
Established:	1993
Transactions:	80-100 annually
GCI:	500,000+

Back in the mid '90's a couple months into getting my real estate license, I was driving down the road and pulled up behind a dark blue Mercedes. The license plate read: PROSPCT

I sped up, pulled alongside to take a look, and it ended up being someone I've known since 7th grade. Bill Watson had also gotten into the real estate business (but a couple of years before me).

Fast forward 20 years to Bill's current real estate practice:

- 80-100 transactions a year (up to 105 a year), year after year, after his first five years in business. He has averaged 80 or more transactions per year since the late '90s.

- Works 222 days and takes 143 days off per year.

- Solo agent with no assistants.

- Has 759 people in his People Portfolio.

- He calls them three times per year and mails them something meaningful four times per year.

- 90% of his business is directly from his Portfolio. Bill averages 10% penetration year after year and has had as high as 16% of his portfolio refer or repeat in a single year.

Bill is one of the top agents in the country. His story encapsulates everything espoused in this book. He built a foundation, operates from his "why" and takes time to rejuvenate and pursue what he loves.

But he is not one of those Mega Agent Ego Driven Superstars – in fact, he's soft spoken and somewhat shy. He's not a tech-guru – he still has an AOL email address (seriously). He could care less about twitter. He doesn't spend a massive amount on advertising or promise his clients '72' things he'll do for them. He just promises to get the job done and his clients trust him.

His philosophy is simple. And his portfolio trusts him completely.

"I keep my promises. I show up on time.
I do what I say I'm going to do".
– Bill Watson

Is Bill's philosophy remarkable? For most people, no, because it's empty. For Bill, yes, because it's true, and his People Portfolio believes it with absolute certainty. His clients trust him and count on him and he delivers. If his clients call him with an urgent question, it matters not if it's 6 a.m. or 10 p.m., he answers or calls back nearly immediately. Bill asks, "Why should my clients have to carry anxiety for a night's sleep or through the weekend if it's a simple thing I can call right back on?"

Are you understanding Bill's 'why'?

Sorry... no magic beans

Agents in the area are always trying to figure out Bill's secrets. Everyone is looking for 'magic beans,' or the quick road to what took Bill years to build. From the outside, agents see tactics.

- Bill gets in the office by 7:30 and is usually home by 5:30
- He started his career knocking on 135 doors a day, 5 days a week. If you do the math, that totals 30,000 doors a year for the first 3 years. Bill still knocks now, but not as often or consistently as in the past.

What envious agents don't see is the "behind the scenes" of everything Bill does.

- He maintains a robust People Portfolio, connects with them often and with authenticity

- He's involved in multiple charities and scholarship funds and is a member of the St. John Bosco Advisory Board

- Has coached over a dozen children's teams. He performs vigorous exercise three times a week and eats mindfully.

- Stays in contact with hundreds of agents he's met across the country

- He takes a lot of time off to rejuvenate

Bill is a craftsman. He gives great care and attention to the smallest of details and ignores the noise of what doesn't matter. To build a business like Bill's takes time, it takes a lot of work. It requires authenticity. There are no shortcuts. But it's achievable by any of us.

If someone has accomplished a success before, you too can do it – they've proven that it's possible. Belief is at the heart of everything, and with the deep understanding that you can have a sustainable business, the universe makes way. It's possible – go do it.

THE RISE OF THE REAL ESTATE CRAFTSMAN

"Success demands singleness of purpose."
– Vince Lombardi

As always, real estate isn't going to be the same tomorrow as it is today. You have no control over this. And while you can't predict the future, you can nonetheless peer slightly ahead by examining trends occurring and emerging now in the broader culture.

Although the business environment changes over time, current trends point to the emergence in the West of the artisan movement, as the fruits of mass production have improved our lives yet left us with the feeling that we are living a carbon copy of our neighbor's life. Our culture is turning to artisans and craftspeople as the key to unlocking the shackles of that hollow feeling.

Instead of just Bud Light, you can choose a higher quality seasonal, small-batch IPA from 21st Amendment in San Francisco; rather than a Hershey bar, you can enjoy fair trade, gourmet chocolate from Escazu in Raleigh.

Beer and chocolate are two well-established boutique industries, but other niches are emerging, too, including fitness, farming, restaurants, and even software. Often hyperlocal and intentionally small, independent producers are sought out for their expressions of passion and originality, whatever the wares.

Perhaps we'll see in coming years the growth of independent artisanal brokerages, piggy-backing the infrastructure of the traditional "big box" real estate brands.

Indeed, one of the biggest problems an agent faces is too *broad* of a focus. Some obvious and common overreaching includes trying to work an area too large to "know," and working disproportionally on marketing initiatives at the expense of relationships. But some well-intentioned labors are just as harmful. You can replicate your marketing message to excess (constant communicating, be it via email, social networks, phones, text messaging, etc.), becoming canned and robotic. When it comes to conversation, quality trumps quantity, and as the Internet highlights the number of options consumers now have, more are turning to higher quality options, even if slightly more expensive.

The phrase, "jack of all trades, master of none" has been in existence for nearly 300 years, yet rings true to this day. The most successful companies operate with a laser focus.

Apple is the canonical example. It doesn't try to fill every computer niche—Apple does not sell netbooks, low-end personal computers or displays, nor printers—but instead designs and produces very few products, each one beautiful, well-made, high-functioning, and wildly popular. Apple operates with an artisanal mindset, focusing on quality. A narrower focus allows you to do a better job, to allow your passion to flow through your work, and ultimately, puts you in a position to actually **be** better than anyone else in your area of specialty.

Speaking of, what is your area of specialty? Can you express it concisely? If not, we challenge you to consider your priorities. What part of your career motivates you to wake up in the morning? Is it working with young buyers to buy new construction or listing high end homes in a specific neighborhood? Ask yourself what is most important to you? What can you forego? How do you spend your time? Is your time allocated according to your core focus? What must change to realign your effort with what's critical, to focus on what you are most passionate about?

You need not and cannot change everything overnight. Slowly do less, omitting one thing at a time. Simplify, simplify, simplify, and your work will be transformed. When you do less, a funny thing happens: you become free to create, to become more like an artisan than one of the ridiculous real estate zombie agents regurgitating each others' website copy. You remain true to your purpose and your passion, and you become more like the highly sought after San Francisco IPA than watered-down Bud Light.

Rest assured, no matter the permutations in real estate, you can adapt through any change as long as you remain connected with your "why" and remain focused on relationships. Ideally, you can team up with a handful of colleagues or partners who are equally as passionate. A small force, focused on pinpoint objectives can do wonderful things and provide an environment that not only sparks and shares energy and inspiration, but also lends you the infrastructure to allow you to rejunvenate and connect with the people that matter to you most.

ABOUT REALVOLVE

A sustainable real estate business begins and ends with people. Connecting, engaging, and growing relationships is the one truth that is, and will remain, timeless.

Frustrated with clunky, bloated, expensive contact management systems built for agents, the founders of Realvolve sketched out an idea for a simple, elegant, easy-to-use CRM, our cocktail napkin moment.

It took a full two bootstrapped years to build our platform from the ground up. Realvolve is on a mission and we're bound to a responsibility in everything we put out, from the aesthetic and behavioral quality of our product to every word we speak and write, because products used every day have an effect on people and their well-being.

We are a company of craftsman and artisans. We are passionately dedicated to providing the environment and the access to the tools, ideas and resources to help our community build quality, sustainable, predictable businesses that fuel fulfilling lives.

ABOUT AGBEAT

Business is fascinating as are emerging technologies, how businesses are adapting, developing, and growing in this new digital economy. The American Genius, est. 2006, is a digital news organization that has chronicled small businesses, startups, and the advancement of digital technology for its early adoptive audience.

AG is completely built using social media to entice an audience with our same passions for the digital evolution in business. We deliver honest, up-to-the-minute coverage of the changing tides, new technologies, new companies, and the opportunities to interact with developing brands.

We reject any news story or editorial column that isn't relevant or high quality, and we reject the premise that a regurgitated press release or old idea is worthy of your time. We hand craft every single story from start to finish, and it shows.

ACKNOWLEDGMENTS

To our families who have supported all of our crazy ideas over the years. And to the thousands of agents, brokers, clients, and friends who have been teachers to us. You have inspired us to package what we've learned and dedicate our lives to helping others. The following people we owe a debt of gratitude, some we've met, some we haven't, but each have been transformative, inspirational figures in our lives.

Joe Polish

Brad Inman

Bill Woolf

Robert Orendain

Yasu Kizaki

David Weltsch

Allen Robinson

Mark Stepp

Terry Hunefeld

Marc Davison

Krisstina Wise

Steven & Shannon Laffoon

Mary La Meres

Lyle Martin

Joe Stumpf

Steve Jobs

Warren Buffet

Timothy Ferriss

Tony Hsieh

Leo Babauta

Anthony Bourdain

David Goodenberger

Rohan Daxini

SPECIAL THANKS

As we go through life certain people weave in and out that leave an impact. One of those people for me was Joe Polish, my roommate when I was 20 years old. Joe, although it took some time to sink in, your 'tough love' changed the trajectory of my life and helped me evolve. You were a beacon of hope and strength and introduced me to a whole new world of writers, marketers and philosophy. Although we've lost touch through the years, I'm grateful for the lessons and imprints.

— Dave Crumby

I would like to thank my business mentor, business partner, and husband, Benn Rosales for an trillion reasons, a few of which I would like to outline in this section.

The very reason I got involved in co-authoring this amazing work of art is not just because Benn encouraged me, offered time off of work (and life) to focus, but because of a single moment we spent together in the ICU years ago. After suffering nine consecutive heart attacks in the emergency room, the calm after the storm created my most cherished moment in life. Rules be damned, I crawled into bed with my husband, we held each other, and he slipped in and out of consciousness while we watched television, desperately grasping at any normalcy.

What that moment in the ICU instilled in me is that you can't wait. You can't wait to write that book, you can't wait to take that trip, you can't wait to improve. You have to do it now. And you have to do it with purpose because life is more meaningful than any single moment can represent.

Fast forward several years, and my husband is a monster in the gym and tougher than ever, but in our moment of private weakness, we became infinitely strengthened and our awareness of life's opportunities were forever magnified.

Benn has been my mentor since I was 20, and taught me how to smile when I'm on the phone (despite my crippling fear of calls), how to carry myself with grace when under fire, and how to balance ambition with patience. He gave me the backbone I have today by believing in me, giving me latitude to make any decision with our company that I want, and for always trusting my gut as I do his.

While I have endless people to thank for my blessings, Benn is why I accomplished most of my life goals before 30 and get to wake up every day to a career and life that I absolutely love.

— Lani Rosales

I'd like to thank my wife, Paige, for her infinite patience. I cannot imagine life without her.

I also have to shout out to my mom, Helene, who taught me how to write good.

— Martin Streicher

ABOUT THE ART

The artwork on pages 33, 41, and 43 provided by Joey Roth.

Prints available at joeyroth.com

ABOUT
DAVE CRUMBY

Dave Crumby is CEO and Co-Founder of Realvolve. Prior to this he was an agent and broker for 15 years. He resides in Denver, Colorado with his wife Lisa and has 4 daughters. Dave enjoys Crossfit, Longboarding, Mountain Biking, Hiking, Tacos and occasionally a few sips of tequila.

ABOUT
LANI ROSALES

Lani Rosales is the Chief Operating Officer of AGBeat.com and the co-founder of TheBashh.com, Lani has been repeatedly named one of real estate's 100 Most Influential Leaders by Inman News, and has been named one of the 12 Most Influential Women in Blogging. She is a business and tech writer hailing from the weird city of Austin. As a digital native, Lani is immersed not only in advanced technologies and new media, but also often buried in piles of reports and stats. Lani prefers beer to your fancy cocktails or sippy drinks.

ABOUT
MARTIN STREICHER

Martin Streicher's professional life has been diverse and colorful. Martin started his career as a Unix system software developer, programming application, utility, and graphics software for timeshared supercomputers. Next, he spent ten years developing entertainment software for personal computers for Berkeley Systems. He was the technical director for the award-winning *After Dark 3.0 Screen Saver* and was the technical director & producer for the first and many subsequent *YOU DON'T KNOW JACK* CD-ROM games.

Martin was the Editor-in-Chief of the national monthly periodical *Linux Magazine* for five years, and was the founding columnist for the popular, long-running "Speaking Unix" column on IBM developerWorks. He has written over a hundred technical articles for Apple, Amazon, and other companies and publications, and has edited books on PHP and Git. For the last five years, Martin has developed software for startups in Ruby on Rails.

Most recently, Martin founded Realvolve with Dave Crumby and serves as its Chief Technology Officer and Chief Operating Officer. Martin has a Master of Science and Bachelor of Science in Computer Science from Purdue University.

A WORD
BEFORE YOU GO

Thank you for investing your time to read this book. I am deeply humbled at this collection of work from some of the wisest and most thoughtful leaders in the industry. It's been a distinct honor to collaborate with them. But growth and progress doesn't stop here.

Six hundred years ago the Dalai Lama advised, ***"Share your knowledge. It's a way to achieve immortality."***

When we focus on sharing our truths from what we learn and practice, the old saying that "a rising tide lifts all boats" rings true and we all share in the benefits.

Please visit RealFWD.com/YOU to continue the conversation, continue learning, and to share how you've put the ideas of this book into practice and how it has changed your business and life.

And with that said, Onward!

Made in the USA
San Bernardino, CA
14 April 2014